**W9-BAL-846**

# Look
# Listen
# Love

## My Faith Trip
## In Europe

## Alisa K. Brown

Look, Listen, Love: My Faith Trip in Europe
© 2011 Alisa K. Brown. All rights reserved.
ISBN 978-1-105-39812-4

Please note that the views and opinions expressed herein
represent my own, and do not reflect those of Barnabas
European Ministries or any other individual or
organization. For more information, please contact me at:
abrown@barnabaseuropeanministries.org.

# Table of Contents

# Introduction
## My Call to Europe

*Expect great thing from God. Attempt great things for God.*
*William Carey*

I was born in Hereford, Texas, some of the flattest landscape in all the world. I remember looking out at the featureless plains and thinking "I've got to get out of here." I couldn't have been more than six years old. It was a strange thought for a little girl who had never been anywhere else. I couldn't possibly have known that my first move (to the San Francisco Bay Area) would be the beginning of a lifetime of moving from place to place. In fact, I have never lived in one place for more than seven years my whole life.

I remember the first time I saw a picture of Europe (I think it was Austria). I was about 12 years old, and my immediate reaction was: "I've got to go live there," not visit, *live*. Again, a strange thought for a young girl who had never been outside of the US.

From my earliest memories, I remember feeling that there was something special, something important for my life: a purpose and a high calling. Again, a strange thought for a little girl who couldn't have been more average or ordinary. Everything about me: my life, my circumstances, my family, my place in the world, testified to nothing special. And in fact, that is the truth. There is nothing special about me except the fact that I've been called by God. A prophet recently told me that I was called from the womb like Jeremiah (Jeremiah 1:5) ". . . set apart for a special work" (NCV)[1].

Of course, I didn't know that I was called until 1999. I was having my regular Bible and prayer time when God suddenly spoke as an audible voice in my head: "Ask Me for it." I opened one eye and gazed toward the ceiling, "Um, ask You for what?" Then I remembered Psalm 37:4: "Take delight in the Lord, and He will give you the desires of your heart." God was inviting me to ask Him for the desire of my heart! Instantly I responded: "OK, Lord, I want to live in Europe." At the time I was a housewife living in Connecticut with my husband and my ten year old son. Of all the houses I've ever lived in, that was the prettiest. And of all the places I had lived, I enjoyed that sweet little town best. I was happy living there. But a desire to live in Europe burned in my heart, as it had done since I was 12. There was no evidence to believe that I could ever live in Europe, but I knew two things: I knew that moving to Europe would take prayer, and lots of it. I also knew that implicit in the invitation was a promise to deliver. So for two years I prayed about moving to Europe. Then my husband was offered a job in Milan, Italy, and we moved there at the end of July 2001.

Although my call to Europe was clear, I still didn't know exactly what to do. I lived in Milan for seven years. Just after my son graduated high school and returned to the US, my husband was laid off. In June of 2007 we moved back to the US, and a year and a half later, we divorced.

Upon separation, I had gone to live with my brother in Bastrop, Texas. There I found a great church. Between

---

[1]  Unless otherwise noted all Bible verses cited are from the New International Version.

church and the friends I met through my brother and sister-in-law, I soon found myself surrounded by loving family and friends. I found a pretty house in the historic district downtown, and again all the elements for happiness were there. But I missed Italy like a distant lover. I tried to content myself by making my environment as Italian as possible. I filled my house with pictures of Italy, I rented only Italian movies, and listened to Italian music.

In February of 2010 I made a trip back to Italy. Becky[2], an American missionary, introduced my by e-mail to a friend of hers, Mary. Mary is from South Africa and does prophetic dance ministry. Since dance was a big part of my life as a young girl, I was fascinated. I had never heard of prophetic dance.

Mary invited me to stay with her in Venice. While I was with her, I asked Mary about prophetic dance. She showed me some videos of her dances. As I watched, fascinated, I felt worship rising for God, who has many, many mysterious ways. Prophetic dance! Only God would come up with something so creative and beautiful. The anointing of the Holy Spirit was clearly upon her, and as she danced, goose bumps danced on my flesh.

In the aftermath of the divorce, I had encountered a lot of trouble praying. I would close my eyes and like a dog with a bone, my mind would keep returning to the divorce. The strategy I used was to pray in a journal. So that evening I prayed for Mary and for her ministry, writing the prayer in

---

[2]  Becky is not her real name. Note that all missionary names have been changed to protect their identities. Many of their locations have also been changed to protect their ministries.

my journal. The following morning I told Mary that I had prayed for her and her ministry. "Really?" she asked. She explained to me that there in Venice she felt very isolated. Her church was 3 hours away (2 by train and 1 by boat), and to her knowledge there was nobody praying for her or her ministry. So I opened the prayer journal and read her the prayer. She was so moved that she asked for a copy of the prayer.

The day I left Venice, I suddenly understood that what I had done for Mary was my ministry. About 20 years earlier I had taken a Spiritual Gifts test, and discovered that I have the gift of encouragements. My interest in and prayers for Mary and her ministry had greatly encouraged her. I felt an urgency to move back to Italy as soon as possible, and get out there and encourage missionaries. When I returned to the US, I immediately started the process of getting my visa. What had taken seven month the first time I moved to Italy, I was able to accomplish in only two. God was opening doors for me.

The other thing I did upon my return to the US was to start a missions organization to encourage and support missionaries and local churches[3] in Europe. Barnabas European Ministries (BEM—not affiliated with any other Barnabas organization) was granted 501c(3) tax-exempt status in record time. What our lawyers told us could take up to two years, actually only took a few months. Again,

---

[3] Barnabas European Ministries (BEM) supports churches and missionaries regardless of denomination or their sending organization. The one thing we look for is a belief in salvation by Jesus Christ. We avoid all other issues and denominational differences because they are potentially divisive. BEM works to unify the Body of Christ.

doors were opening. BEM was created to minister encouragement and support through Prayer, Hospitality, and Collaboration.

On 1 May 2010 I moved back to Milan with my cat, Boo-Boo. My first year in ministry I spent almost entirely in Italy, getting legally settled, re-established with my community of friends and church family, and connecting with missionaries, and giving them encouragement and prayer support. I realized that living in Milan the first time with my family had been very useful in aiding my return. The daunting tasks of getting a permit to stay, residency, identity card, etc. were not new to me. Plus I was already fluent in Italian, and knew the many different measurements here (temperature in Celsius, metric measurements, the Euro, etc.). Not only that, but I was now in a position to help other missionaries with these issues.

## Italy[4]

Only 15% (and possibly as low as 3%) of Italians are practicing Catholics, and of those, many practice a superstitious Catholicism, and pray to Padre Pio or Saint Anthony. One of the global centers for Satanism is in Turin, and there are more than 150,000 practicing soothsayers, prognosticators, and healers. There are more Jehovah's Witnesses than all Protestants in Italy combined. Pray to remove the barriers that limit understanding of the Gospel. (Operation World, pgs. 481-485.)

---

[4] All country facts cited throughout the book are taken from Operation World 7th Edition, Jason Mandryk, 2010.

## Holy See (Vatican)

Many issues continue to divide the world's largest religious body: ecumenism, celibacy of the priesthood, the position of women, homosexuality and AIDS, and contraception. The Church has also lost a lot of credibility due to numerous scandals.

Pray for spiritual renewal, a return to Biblical truths, and for unscriptural practices and beliefs to be formally and finally dropped by the Church and its enormous flock. (Operation World, pgs. 396-397.)

## Prologue
## The Motive for the Faith Trip

*"Every place that the sole of your foot will tread upon I
have given you . . ."*
*Joshua 1:3a (NKJV)*

After living in my apartment in Milan for six months,
through an odd series of circumstances, I felt led to give
notice on my apartment. As soon as I did, God spoke to my
spirit, saying, "I have a house for you." Because Milan is
strategically located, and because I know the city very
well, I began hunting for an apartment to buy—no more
throwing money away on rent. I had six months to find a
place before I had to get out of the apartment. But I found
nothing suitable. I saw the ugliest apartments, in
neighborhoods I would never walk through alone at night.
Finally I found an apartment in a well-connected suburb. It
was small, but otherwise perfect. I made an offer. The
sellers didn't respond. In fact, they immediately took the
apartment off the market. Could there be a firmer NO than
that? And by then my move-out date was frighteningly
close.

Clearly something had gone wrong, so I prayed, asking
God why I hadn't found the house He has for me. He said,
"You never asked Me." Then He showed me that I needed
to take a Faith Trip and head out into the rest of my mission
field: Europe. I call it a Faith Trip because only God knew
the exact itinerary. My heart beat so hard I thought it was
going to wake the neighbors. I was terrified, but also
excited. I am always up for an adventure, and God has
shown me that with the right attitude, life is full of
adventure. I understood that this was going to be as
important for the ministry as it would be for me. This was

God's training school so that I could learn to follow His leading more closely. It's humbling to publicly admit this failing. I have a lot of faith, but I have always had a tendency to run ahead of God. So the personal objective of the Faith Trip would be to learn to temper faith with wisdom and to wait upon the Lord.

Wait! If passing the test depended on an ability to wait, fear of failure was as frightening as the idea of not knowing my next move. The most frightening thing about not knowing the itinerary was the thought that I might be sleeping in parks or train stations. I pleaded with God to provide a bed or a couch to sleep on. He gently reassured me that He would provide me with a place to sleep each night.

The one and only thing I knew before the Faith Trip was the starting point: Hope For Europe (also called Hope 2), a conference for missionaries in Europe that I would be attending. Hope 2 would be held in Budapest, Hungary.

What follows is the day-by-day story of my Faith Trip. I could never have imagined the places it took me, the wonders I saw, the myths destroyed, or the lessons learned. It is my prayer that each of you reading this will also grow in your faith, knowledge, and love for God. And if you feel the call to Europe as I did, I pray that you will answer it. Europe needs more missionaries to carry the hope and love of Jesus Christ to a whole generation of the least-reached people group in the western world: the European youth.

## Europe

The last 250 years have seen worldwide advance for the gospel, but decline in Europe, such that today's European youth can be called the "least reached" people group.

Ironically, this continent which was once the home of Christianity and sender of missionaries to the rest of the world has instead become secular. Criminality is rampant, especially human trafficking, which has been made much easier by the relaxation of border controls between most European nations. Freedom of public religious expression is eroding, making evangelism extremely difficult. Practical atheism or a fuzzy spirituality are the dominant belief systems among Europeans. Immigration and higher birthrates have made Islam the second religion of Europe, and the fastest-growing religion on the continent.

Pray for revival across Europe, for creative, innovative, and relational evangelism, and for more workers for this vast and forgotten mission field. (Operation World, pgs. 72-81.)

## Faith Trip - Day 0
## Before the Faith Trip

*Beware in your prayers, above everything else, of limiting God, not only by unbelief, but by fancying that you know what He can do. Expect unexpected things "above all that we ask or think."*
*Andrew Murray*

Before anyone else knew about the Faith Trip, God gave me Joshua 1:1-10. Three times in this passage God tells Joshua (and me!): "Be strong and courageous." Four of my friends, upon hearing about the Faith Trip, gave me those same words from Joshua, which was powerfully encouraging confirmation.

Pietro and Marta, missionary friends in Tuscany, upon hearing about the Faith Trip, invited me to come stay with them a few days before I leave. They introduced me to other missionaries who know about people throughout Italy that host missionaries for free or at a nominal fee. Together with the few that I already knew about, I could see a hospitality network growing.

As a going-away present, Pietro gave me Vagabonda per il Signore, the Italian translation of Corrie ten Boom's book, Tramp for the Lord. In his husky baritone Pietro told me, "It occurs to me that, just like Corrie ten Boom, you will also be a tramp for the Lord, traveling into your old age." Then he threw a fatherly arm around my shoulders (although we're the same age) and smiled.

This was confirmation of two prophecies I received months before I ever knew about the Faith Trip, one of which said: "You are about to start traveling. Pack carefully and travel light." I have to admit that the idea of

10

traveling into my old age is not one that thrilled me at first. Travel is exhausting. But at the same time, I know that I have been specially equipped for travel in a couple of very important ways: First, I learned many years ago to always carry a book and a notebook with me. With these, I can become so engrossed in reading or writing that time waiting for and on trains or flights passes quickly. Second, I have the ability to sleep anytime, anywhere in a seated position. If I'm not driving, a car on the highway becomes a sleeping pill for me. And with regard to sleep, I benefit as much from a 20 minute nap as most people benefit from an hour. I can fully regenerate in five hours a night, though six is ideal. It is very rare that I sleep more than seven hours. And I find couches more comfortable than beds, which is also handy for someone traveling and staying with people in various places and circumstances. Given the choice of a couch or a bed, I always choose the couch.

At the train station Pietro and Marta prayed for me with the sound of passing trains almost carrying the sound of their voices away. Pietro prayed that I would feel at home wherever I go because God is my home. As he prayed this, I really did understand that God is my home. I began in that moment to feel the love and care and security of being always at home with God. And with that, I began to feel ready to head out into the unknown adventure of this Faith Trip.

I returned to Milan. I had given up my apartment, so I went to stay with Pina and Luigi for the last few nights leading up to the conference in Budapest. Boo-Boo, my cat, was living with the Stefanelli family, whose children loved her at first sight. Being "homeless" was scary, but also incredibly freeing. I knew that this would be an ideal time to be traveling. Having made the decision to embrace the adventure and not worry about the unknown, I was excited to start the Faith Trip. Jesus taught us not to worry about the piddly details of our lives (Matthew 6:25-34). So, I decided to leave the details and the unknown to the only One who could possibly know and do something about it.

Two days before leaving on the Faith Trip I had some errands to run. I prayed about these errands before leaving the house. It was soon obvious that I had somehow gone wrong again because the bank was closed (on a weekday!), and I was not able to connect with any of the people I had wanted to see before leaving town. I had gone off, head in the clouds, and missed whatever God had for me that day. I had prayed first! I hadn't done anything sinful or overtly wrong. But one of the chief complaints of my teachers throughout school was that I was a daydreamer. I had stepped out the door and quickly gone on autopilot, daydreaming and missing the lesson my Teacher had for me that day.

Nobody is more grateful for a second chance than I am! And nobody knows better than I that God is the God of a Second Chance. This morning I also prayed about my errands before heading out. As I prayed, I confessed my desperation and need for Him. Desperation suddenly was replaced by an otherworldly calm as I understood that it's very simple: all I have to do is Look, Listen, and Love. Look at the people and things around me. Listen for His instructions. Let Love be my highest motivation. So I went out to do these important last things, with the intention to Look, Listen, and Love.

First, I needed to go to the bank, and this would be my last chance before leaving town. This time it was open. As I exited the bank, there in front of me was the number nine tram. This tram wouldn't take me exactly where I needed to go next, but it would take me within a few blocks. I didn't know why, but I felt the Holy Spirit urging me to take this tram. The Italian term for this urging is *un spinto dello Spirito Santo*, a "push" of the Holy Spirit. And it did feel like a gentle push. So I got onto the tram. A few stops later a man got on and I heard a familiar deep voice greeting me—it was Alberto, a friend from the prayer team at my Italian church. He asked about my trip, and then promised to pray for me in intercessory prayer the following morning. I hadn't had a chance to remind them to pray for my trip. This, I realized was a Divine Appointment.

When I got off the tram, I started walking toward the next thing I needed to do. As I passed in front of the grocery store, the face of Gessica, a good friend, suddenly came to mind. I hadn't seen her for some months, so I pulled out the phone to call her. I don't think in pictures, so picture thoughts are almost always from God. Over familiar background noise, I heard Gessica say that she was too busy to talk at the moment. I said, "Where are you?" and she said she was at the grocery store. I told her, "I'm right outside!" So I helped her carry her groceries home. She made lunch for me and prayed for my trip. She also said that she would have her cell group pray for me tomorrow evening. As I left her house, Gessica said, "Watch for God's hand at work, Listen for His voice, and Go where He directs you with Love in your heart." My jaw dropped open. It was confirmation of Look, Listen, Love! Clearly this was Divine Appointment number two.

This morning I got a phone call from Bethany, who I had met at a conference in Rome. She had been living in the UK at the time. But the day I met her, she had also met a pastoral couple from a small town in northern Italy. She

13

knew right away that the Holy Spirit was telling her that she needed to come to Italy to help them and their church. So after the conference Bethany went back to the UK, quit her job, sold her house and virtually all of its contents, and moved to Italy—a bold leap into the unknown. We hadn't talked since Rome, but I had sent her a message about the Faith Trip. Bethany had called to say that she wanted to see me before my departure. I told her it was today or nothing. So I met her at the train station and we spent the rest of the day together, catching up with the last several months and giggling like little girls. It was such fun! Then Bethany bought me dinner and prayed for me and for the Faith Trip. It was my third Divine Appointment.

At last I feel ready to jump off into the unknown. Early tomorrow morning my flight takes off for Budapest. Adventure, here I come!

## Hungary

The atheistic Communists placed strict controls on all Christians from 1948 - 1988, using discrimination, intimidation, and infiltration. The openness of the post-Communist 1990's has passed, and now it is forbidden for teachers, doctors, and other professionals to share the Christian faith in the workplace.

Pray for revival and boldness to speak about Jesus, and for openness and receptivity to the Good News. (Operation World, pgs. 400-403.)

## Faith Trip - Day 1
## Hope for Europe

*The Great Commission is not an option to be considered; it is a command to be obeyed.*
*Hudson Taylor*

The conference is called Hope for Europe or Hope 2, being the second meeting of Hope for Europe. This is the start point for the Faith Trip—the only thing I know about the itinerary.

I arrived at Budapest's enormous Conference Center about an hour before registration. Even though it was early in the day and early for registration, there was already a buzz of activity and lots of people scurrying about. The first person I met was Katie, a missionary from Louisiana who is working with a missions organization in Budapest. I told Katie about a mix-up when my Italian rental agreement was sent to Bastrop, Louisiana instead of Bastrop, Texas. The rental agreement was an essential document. Without it I would never have gotten my Italian Visa. She knew both Bastrops and laughed. Bastrop, Louisiana is tiny. It's amazing that anyone would have mixed them up. Her bright brown eyes and ready grin confirmed that she's here to facilitate registration. We exchanged contact information. I have a feeling I will be seeing more of Katie.

Once registered, people began arriving by the dozens. The conference got underway. I started right in networking at lunch and between plenary sessions. I learned a lot about the Christian roots of Europe. Paul's vision of the man pleading for him to come to Macedonia (Europe) is still Europe's plea to missionaries. People came to the conference from all around the world, leaving their homelands to answer that plea. I met an artist from Australia, a pastor from India, an intercessor from Ghana, a nurse from Costa Rica and many, many Americans. These people are all laboring in the European mission fields, working with children, students, businesses, the elderly, gypsies, Muslims, churches, schools, governments—all of European society—to bring the love of Jesus to a continent that has forgotten its Christian roots.

In the first plenary session we learned about Robert Schuman, the visionary French Foreign Minister whose declaration of 9 May 1950 established the European Union. Schuman wrote:

> We are called to bethink ourselves of the Christian basics of Europe by forming a democratic model of governance which through reconciliation develops into a "community of peoples" in freedom, equality, solidarity and peace and which is deeply rooted in Christian basic values.

Given that Europe is "deeply rooted in Christian basic values," it is shocking to see its decline into humanism, atheism, and nihilism. That Europe is hungry for a spiritual reality is evident in its embrace of the New Age, Dianetics (Scientology), neo-paganism, Jehovah's Witnesses, Buddhism, Mormonism, and even Satanism. Just like hungry children will reach for a cookie instead of a healthy meal, Europeans starved for a spiritual life lack the discernment to know the good from the harmful.

I enjoyed the first day of the conference, but I'm

exhausted. The two kilometer walk back to the hotel woke me up enough to write down these thoughts, but now I'm done. My roommate hasn't shown up yet, but I've got to get to bed.

## Albania

Albania is one of the poorest nations in Europe. Communism left Albania economically, morally, and spiritually devastated.   Islam is the largest religion.

Pray for committed missionaries to come serve in Albania. Pray also that Albania's poverty will lead more to seek and trust Jesus. (Operation World, pgs. 94-97.)

## Faith Trip - Day 2
## More Hope for Europe

*The man who mobilizes the Christian church to pray will make the greatest contribution to world evangelization in history.*
*Andrew Murray*

At breakfast I finally met my roommate, Julia. She is a missionary from South Africa, serving in Austria. She told me hesitatingly about her interest in having an arts ministry and outreach programs. She paints, so I asked to see a painting, which she showed me on her computer back in our room after breakfast. It was beautiful, colorful, and full of life. It appeared to me that the only thing she was missing was confidence, and I told her so.

Julia's eyes then filled with tears as she opened up and told me about some difficulties she was having in her marriage. I grabbed a box of tissues, prayed for her, and promised to continue praying for her marriage. Marriages are under attack, especially couples in ministry. Many people these days, if they marry at all, marry with the idea that if things don't work out they can always divorce. Of course Christians embrace a more permanent view of marriage, but that doesn't make Christian marriages immune to break-ups. Husbands are sometimes enticed away by a pretty young woman or wives by a man who pays her more attention. Sometimes arguments over silly things get blown out of all proportion, escalating into all-out war—or worse, silence. Unity within the Body of Christ must begin with unity within marriages. Open communication, honesty, and prayer are important weapons in defense of marriage. It is no shame to be tempted—even Jesus was tempted. It is also not shameful (or even unusual) to encounter problems in relationships. Put any two people together and sooner or later they will find something they disagree about. The important thing is to maintain communication, even when it's difficult to admit to the problem. In fact, that's probably when it's most important to communicate. As I shared these thought with Julia, she agreed that she needed to have a long talk with her husband when she returns to Austria. I told her, "I think you two will be able to get past this little bump. And your marriage will be stronger for it." She smiled and hugged me.

Then I headed back to the Conference Center alone. Julia wanted to wash her hair. This second day of the conference was more networking and more learning about Europe and its unique situation. For example, today we learned that in order to sustain a stable population, there must be a 2.1% rate of fertility. Throughout the native European population the fertility rate ranges from 2.0 to as low as .8%. In addition, the countries with the highest suicide rates in the world are in Europe: Belarus, Lithuania, and Russia, and "suicide tourism" makes Switzerland the top one-way destination in the world. Is it any wonder that the native European population is in decline? Immigration and a far higher birthrate makes Islam the fastest-growing religion throughout Europe. The result is isolated and aging Europeans plus young, breeding immigrants equals the population mix of today's Europe, and a peek at what tomorrow's Europe will look like. However, the Bible is incredibly inclusive—all of us have sinned and need salvation. We cannot afford to let these facts cause us to despair, but instead to inspire us to action. A whole mission field has arrived upon Europe's doorstep, and this is an opportunity we can't afford to miss.

Between sessions I looked through the area set up for the various networks, some of which were selling books. I met the people in charge of the Disabilities Network, and was astonished to learn how non-inclusive most church services are. It's not only a matter of a lack of ramps and elevators, but also the music and the sermons fail to engage those with learning disabilities, hearing problems, and mental handicaps. For example, one man told me about how confusing it is for people with these kinds of difficulties to understand when we sing "He reigns." He told me of one young man who thought it meant that Jesus was in the rainclouds. How could we let these dear people be overlooked?

To be honest, by the evening session I was so tired, and the facts had been flying at me so fast all day, that I began to miss some of the things that were said by the speakers. I even caught myself dozing off a couple of times. However, I took every opportunity to network throughout the day, and met a lot of really amazing people from all over the world, and in all kinds of ministry.

The walk back to the hotel in the cool, fresh air woke me up again, refreshing me to write these thoughts before I go to bed. Tomorrow we will break off into our networks. Mine is Prayer. Others are: Arts (Julia's Network), Children's Ministries, Church Leaders and Church Planting, Cities (urban ministries), Disabilities, Ethne Europe (reaching out to the marginalized peoples of Europe), Evangelism, GATE - Gifts from Africa To Europe (African missions to Europe!), Health Network, Leadership Development, Muslims in Europe, Politics, Theology, Women in Leadership, and Worship. It's exciting to see God at work in Europe.

## Austria

Most Austrians believe in God—84%, which is high for Europe. But few have a personal relationship with Jesus. There is a lot of cult activity, New Age, Eastern religions, Jehovah's Witnesses (outnumbering evangelicals), Mormons, and the New Apostolic Church. The Dalai Lama conducted a rite releasing 722 spirits to make Austria the bridgehead of Buddhism for Western Europe. And the Catholic, Lutheran, and Reformed churches are in serious decline, especially among the youth.

Pray for a spirit of renewal and revival in the Body of Christ. (Operation World, pgs. 123-126.)

## Faith Trip - Day 3
## Prayer Network

*The history of missions is the history of answered prayer.*
*Samuel Zwemer*

The Prayer Network is made up of people from various ministries, from various countries, and serving in diverse places throughout Europe. Vincent, from the Netherlands, is the facilitator. He stepped in when the original facilitator, Warren, suddenly died a few months ago. I didn't know Warren, but he had obviously been a Spirit-filled man of prayer. Warren's widow attended the conference. Although she was signed up for a different network, she came to the opening session of the Prayer Network. Most of the people there had known Warren, so each took turns sharing with her how Warren had touched their lives. There was laughter sprinkled with tears. Clearly Warren was very much loved and missed. Then we formed a circle around her and prayed for her and for their children.

With the conference ending tomorrow, I began to feel anxious to know where I will be going from here. Due to the lack of a house of prayer in Italy, my partner in ministry has recently become interested in investigating and possibly starting one. Because of her interest, she knew about a couple that would be attending the Prayer Network: Nigel and Fiona, who have started a house of prayer for England. Probably it was my human guess and anxiousness to know the next step that caused me to believe that from Hungary I was supposed to go to England and visit their house of prayer. But when I approached them at lunch with the idea of a visit, they gently discouraged me from visiting—they had other things to do.

My face flushed hot with embarrassment. Obviously, I had gone wrong again. I went back to the room after lunch, spending the rest of the lunch break praying in desperation—and yes, hiding.

In the afternoon session we took turns introducing ourselves, speaking about our ministries, and praying for each person and their ministry. First was Stacy from Slovakia, whose ministry is worship music. In fact, Stacy played the keyboards and led us in a time of worship. Others around the room introduced themselves and their ministries, but Stacy with her impish grin was one person I definitely wanted to know better.

I made it a point to sit with Stacy at dinner—and avoiding Nigel and Fiona, if you really want to know the truth! I tried not to look like I was avoiding them, and Stacy is a delightful girl with a great sense of comic timing. I've never laughed more through a meal than I did tonight with Stacy. It was a tonic after the embarrassing fiasco with Nigel and Fiona. My sides are still aching from laughing so hard and so much. I thanked Stacy for the laughter workout, telling her, "I need more workouts like that!"

At the evening session, the Prayer Network finished the introductions, and mine was one of the last. I explained about my ministry's scope (Europe) and objectives (missionary encouragement and support of local churches) and methods (Prayer, Hospitality, and Collaboration). I received lots of prayers, blessings, and prophecies that night, but none stuck with me more than Klaus's. Klaus is a prophet like Agabus[5] or Hosea, whose prophecies were

---

[5] Acts 21:10-11

acted out. Normally Klaus seems to be a rather fragile old man, but when he approaches someone with a prophecy, as he approached me, he's suddenly powerful. In that moment Klaus could be the personification of Aslan from the Chronicles of Narnia. He fixed me with his large brown eyes and paused for what seemed like almost half a minute. Finally, he held out his hands waist-high and said, "Put your hands in mine." I did, and he turned my hands palms-up. "Relax into my hands." I let my hands rest in his. "No! Really relax the full weight of your arms," he instructed. I let go all the tension in my arms, and Klaus began rocking my hands gently side to side. "The Lord says that you are to rest in Him like this, leaning on Him and trusting Him fully to carry the weight of your burdens for you."

And with that, it's the end of another exhausting, embarrassing, but wonderful day. I still don't know where I to go, but the message is clear: I need to rest in the Lord. He knows what comes next, even if I don't.

### Slovakia

Despite being one of the strongest-growing economies in the EU, there remains in Slovakia, as in other post-Communist countries, a broad economic gap and persistent unemployment. With the end of Communism and subsequent separation from the Czech Republic, have come increasing wealth for some and new influences of materialism and moral relativism. Depression and suicide rates are among the highest in Europe, which is also high worldwide.

Pray for the Slovakian people to find hope in Jesus Christ. (Operation World, pgs. 747-749.)

## Faith Trip - Day 4
## Stepping Out into the Unknown

*To be certain of God means that we are uncertain in all our ways, we do not know what a day may bring forth. This is generally said with a sigh of sadness; it should rather be an expression of breathless expectation.*
*Oswald Chambers*

The conference has ended and everyone is checked out of the hotel—some checked out before breakfast. I still didn't know what to do or where to go next. I've been trying to wait upon the Lord, but the silence from above was almost deafening. There were a couple of things I needed to do while in Budapest, so I decided to go out and do them. In this I was given confirmation when Sarabeth from Switzerland gave me a whole packet of bus tickets. She had planned on seeing more of the city, but simply hadn't had time. And with that decision I felt the nudge of the Holy Spirit to check out of the hotel, too. So I checked out after breakfast, but asked the hotel to hold my bags for me.

I needed to do three things today: one was to meet Steve, a missionary that my ministry partner knows. Via e-mail, Steve had suggested an afternoon meeting. Second, I needed to buy a Hungarian SIM chip for my phone. That way I could call Steve. I also wanted a Hungarian SIM chip so that my family could contact me if they needed me urgently. At least daily I check e-mail, but I have a grandchild on the way and a recently-widowed mother who might need to call me. So it's important to have a local phone so that I can call them, too, if I need to. Although I had seen an advertisement for Vodafone at the airport when I arrived, I hadn't seen a Vodafone store *anywhere*.

26

The third thing I had wanted to do was to visit a church suggested by a friend. I picked the third thing first, thinking that I would see a Vodafone store on the way. At the very least, it would be an adventure.

But once again I ran ahead of God. Nobody at the church was expecting me. The church turned out to be a mega-church and school. It was busy as a beehive with all sorts of activity, and buzzing with dozens of conversations in Hungarian. I looked around, but it was obvious that I would need an appointment if I ever hoped to talk to someone.

Even though I was unsuccessful at making any connection at the church, it was still a valuable opportunity to learn my way around town. I had bought a street map before setting out, which turned out to be incredibly helpful for getting around in Budapest. Struggling to understand the public transportation system without knowing a single word of Hungarian was a challenge. It made me appreciate the ease of understanding Milan's system, which doesn't require a knowledge of Italian or even literacy. In Budapest there seems to be an assumption that you know the language and that you can read (perhaps this means that Hungary has a high literacy rate). There also seems to be an assumption that everyone knows how Budapest is laid out. Before buying the map, here's what I knew about Budapest's geography: Buda is on one side of the Danube and Pest is on the other. Directions for the subway say Ujpest or Kispest. Maybe you know Hungarian or are familiar with Budapest, but without the map I would never have guessed that Ujpest is north Pest and Kispest is south Pest.

I also had a little adventure on a bus. I tried to signal for a stop by pushing the button on the post by the door. It didn't ring so I pushed it again. Meanwhile, the bus sailed past my stop and the next one and the next one. Finally I realized that the button I had pushed was the one for opening the door, which of course doesn't do anything while the bus is in motion. The button to signal a stop was overhead, almost up at the ceiling! It was a reach for me, and I wondered what little people do to signal a stop. When the bus finally stopped I crossed the street and waited for a bus to take me back to my destination. This time I asked the driver, showing him where on the map I wanted to go. He didn't speak English, but he instructed me in Hungarian with lots of gestures. A helpful young man overheard and told me that he said to get off at the second stop and take the number 86 bus. The young man also got off and took the number 86, too. From there, he told me where to get off.

The church had been in far south Pest (Kispest). I still hadn't seen a single Vodafone store the whole way down there. So I stopped in McDonalds to take advantage of their free Wi-Fi. On the internet I discovered that there is only one Vodafone store in Budapest—in far north Pest (this is how I learned Ujpest and Kispest!). So I set out for the other end of town.

I did the same as before, showing the driver my map. At one point, the driver became very concerned when he saw me get up out of my seat before my stop. I was only giving up my seat for an elderly person. All the bus drivers have been very helpful, despite the language barrier. In fact, they seem very eager to help. I think the kindness and helpfulness of the bus drivers more than makes up for the almost incomprehensible public transportation system. I arrived in far north Pest (Ujpest), found the Vodafone store, and bought a SIM chip. I was pleased to see that it works in my phone.

I called Steve and finally, we met. We went to Rézkígyó Kávézó (The Bronze Serpent) Christian Coffeehouse run by YWAM Budapest. We enjoyed some great music there, and who was playing the keyboard? Katie from Louisiana! We exchanged quick greetings between songs. However, Steve and I were not able to stay for long because it was getting late and I still needed to find a place to stay. He told me that his church has an apartment for visiting missionaries and pastors.

About an hour later, I had the keys to their guest house. But I needed to cross town (into Buda) to retrieve my bags from the hotel. And I needed to get back before the trams stopped running. I put the timing into God's hands, praying that I wouldn't lose any time getting lost in the process. I don't fear getting lost by day because I have a pretty good sense of direction if the sun is out to help me. But nighttime is another story. Without the sun to help guide me, I can get very badly turned around, especially if I'm tired. Under those circumstances I've gotten lost even in familiar territory.

I checked the map and saw that the tram that passed in front of the apartment would take me close to the hotel on the other side of the river. It was difficult to see the dark world racing by outside from the tram's brightly-lit interior. After the river I started counting stops. Then a middle-aged woman sat down beside me and wanted to engage me in conversation. I said, "Sorry, I don't speak the language." She switched to English, even more eager to talk with me. I told her that I was sorry, but I needed to watch for my stop. It didn't slow her down a bit. On and on she chattered, nudging me with her elbow every few seconds. I admit, I am not a night-owl, and I was getting cranky. Her incessant blather and that elbow were beginning to get on my nerves. But I also understand and appreciate the desire for someone to talk to, so I tried to set aside my own feelings, and watch for my stop the best I could. Then at one stop, just as the doors were closing, I realized suddenly that it was my stop. I rushed to the door, shouting, "Stop! Stop!" The tram driver opened the door again for me and a cold wind almost knocked me off my feet. All this time, the woman continued chattering away in English as if nothing had happened. I thought, "She's probably still working that elbow, too." Once out of the tram, the doors closed swiftly. I waved at the lady—she had been nice, and lonely, God bless her, even if she had been annoying and distracting. She waved back and then she and the tram were gone, and I felt like a jerk for letting a little conversation and an elbow irritate me. God still has a lot of work to do in me!

I pulled out the map again, trying to get my bearings and figure out which direction I needed to be walking. It was important that I get moving quickly, but even more important that I get moving in the right direction. That cold wind kept blowing from the direction of the river, which helped me get my bearings. After about 10 minutes of walking I found myself in familiar territory, close to the hotel. They had stashed my bags in the room we had used for the meetings of the Prayer Network. I grabbed my bags and bid the night clerk good night.

I followed that same cold wind back to the tram stop. After about 20 minutes a tram came—the last run of the night—and took me back across the river, rejoicing all the way. The apartment was in a much better-lit part of town, so I was able to spot my stop without any trouble. I returned to the apartment and snuggled into bed, grateful to God who loves me and had provided me with a nice place to sleep.

As I was praying this morning I realized an important ministry purpose for this Faith Trip: not just to contact more missionaries and churches, but to put together a list of missionary guest houses. In this expensive mission field, being able to save money on hotels is a major blessing. And since Hospitality is one of the three core means we use to encourage missionaries, having a list of free or low-priced accommodations makes a lot of sense. Little by little I'm learning to wait upon the Lord, and the ministry is advancing at the same time. God is good!

### Andorra, Liechtenstein, & Luxembourg

These three tiny countries are wealthy banking and low-tax havens, with strongly Catholic histories, but freedom of religion. Catholicism has declined into nominalism, secularism, materialism, and fuzzy personalized spirituality, with Islam, Jehovah's Witnesses, and Eastern mysticism advancing alongside Protestant groups.

Pray for true faith to replace all false beliefs, and to overcome the seductions of wealth and materialism. (Operation World, pgs. 539-540; 543-545.)

## Faith Trip - Days 5 & 6
## Bumming Around Budapest

*The spiritual life cannot be made suburban. It is always*
*frontier, and we who live in it must accept and even rejoice*
*that it remains untamed.*
*Howard Macey*

The person in charge of the church's apartment me know
that I would have to check out by Monday morning. I
didn't know where I would be going next, but I decided not
to let that interfere with my weekend—I'm learning! Since
I was down to my last clean change of clothes, I did
laundry first thing yesterday morning, washing everything
by hand in the sink and hanging it all up, dripping over the
bath tub.

With the laundry done and drying, I went to McDonalds to
do some writing and to check e-mail. In the afternoon
when I finished with my writing tasks, I took a walk in the
neighborhood of the Christian Coffeehouse (walking
distance from the apartment). I had seen a Jewish Cultural
Center on the same street and I wanted to check it out. Of
course the Center was closed, being a Saturday, but I saw a
notice on the door inviting all to come to the Israel
Independence Day celebration on Sunday (today). I made a
mental note to return for the celebration after church.

Between these things, the day was mostly gone. I was not
able to see as much of Budapest as I would have liked, but
I'm learning to take care of all my resources wisely,
including strength and energy.

This morning as I prayed about checking out of the guest

house, God revealed to me that I would be invited to the place where I need to go next. With that, I ate breakfast and went to church. The worship music was 90% in Hungarian. I clapped time to the music and concentrated on loving God without worrying about the words. The pastor turned out to be American, so the message was in English with Hungarian translation. The message was excellent—all about being relational in order to share Jesus. He pointed out that being relational means respecting the individual and the person's culture, and responding to the person's needs without sharing in their sin. Emphasis on respect. Great message!

After church I went to the Jewish Heritage Center. I used their free Wi-Fi to check e-mail. The first message I opened was an invitation to come visit a church in Romania. I met the pastor's wife, Clara, at Hope for Europe. She and I felt an immediate connection. I wrote and told her that I need to check out of the guest house tomorrow morning. Happily, she was online and replied immediately with an invitation to come to Romania tomorrow.

By the time I finished my internet work the Israeli Independence Day celebration was in full swing. I was delighted to find that it was being held in the center of a genuine hippy earth-mother crafts market. I love street markets, and crafts markets especially. There were lots of clever, pretty things at very low prices. I bought a soft toy kitty for my unborn grandchild, pleased with the idea of something handmade from Hungary for the baby. In the center of the market was a stage where there were traditional dances, Hebrew songs, and a cooking demonstration—with free samples of the results!

Delicious!

Later in the afternoon I went to the train station to buy my ticket. Google maps had indicated that it would only take about 4-5 hours to drive to north central Romania from Budapest. However, with border crossings and a train change, it was predicted to be more like 11-12 hours by train. The train is cheaper than flying and this way I will be able to see the countryside. Google maps shows that the train goes right along the edge of the Hungarian National Park. So I bought my ticket and headed back to the apartment with a heady sense of tomorrow's adventure: Romania!

On the way back to the apartment I discovered two things: the first was a cathedral that was open. Mass just ending, so I entered and sat down. I like to go into the churches to pray a moment whenever I find them open. When I came out of the church again it had started to rain. To get back to the apartment from I had to go through the outer area of the subway station. This is where I made my second discovery: where the homeless people go when it rains here. There were several homeless people lying head-to-toe against the wall. Budapest has a lot of homeless people—more than Milan or any other city I've ever seen. Operation World estimates as many as 33,000 homeless people in Budapest. That's a small city within the city! The homeless in Budapest mostly don't beg for money. They appear to have given up. You see them lying in doorways and under trees in the park. I had wondered where they go when it's cold or raining. Now I know. And apparently it's OK with the police because there were police right there. There always are police underground in Budapest, and that's probably a good thing.

Tomorrow: Romania! The adventure continues!

## Israel[6]

Israel is well developed in the high-tech, bio-tech, chemical, and agricultural sectors, and hosts many start-up companies. But the expense of defense, security, new immigrants, and the lack of water are a continuing burden. On top of that, Israel lacks natural resources and needs to import petroleum, coal, grains, and military hardware. Issues of poverty and the constant threat of violence and war plague Israel from within and without.

Pray for true reconciliation and genuine Shalom through Jesus the Messiah. (Operation World, pgs. 477-481.)

---

[6] Note: Although my primary focus and call is Europe, I heard a prophecy at Hope for Europe saying, "If you want to win your mission field, you must be willing to look beyond it." I have done exactly that with this entry about how to pray for Israel.

## Faith Trip - Day 7
## Post-Communist Border Crossing

*The Lord had said to Abram, "Leave your country, your*
*people and your father's household and go to the land I*
*will show you."*
*Genesis 12:1*

This is a good time to introduce you to my traveling
companion: Prayer Bear. He's a brown, fuzzy pillow with
a teddy-bear head. He has a button that folds him into a
bearlike shape, allowing him to hold onto the loop at the
top of my backpack. I call him Prayer Bear (or PB for
short) because he's perfect for kneeling on. PB and I spend
time together with God every day, and prayer builds
relationships—even with make-believe playmates, it
seems. He's also useful anytime I need a pillow. PB has a
goofy grin and he makes friends with children, wherever
we go—even here where I don't speak the language. But
he's no ordinary bear/pillow, as I found out today.

The Hungarian National Park is beautiful, big, and green,
but it doesn't offer a variety of views, so soon I fell asleep
on the train (as I frequently do!). I was woken up by the
conductor asking for my ticket. And just after the
conductor passed PB jumped off the overhead shelf and
dangled upside-down, grinning at me. I whipped out my
camera and took a picture, giggling. I'm sure my seatmates
thought I was crazy, but I had fun, so who is really crazy?
(Well, OK, it's *still* me! But who cares?)

A few minutes later I began to drift off again. At the next
station, the train stopped and a border guard asked to see
our passports. When he looked at my American passport,

he grimaced, turned, and got off the train, still holding my passport. I looked around, but mine was the only passport taken. Scenes from <u>God's Smuggler</u> went through my mind, but I decided to do like Brother Andrew did: just relax and let God handle it. Ten long minutes later the border guard brought back my passport and gave it to me.

The train continued on, and I began to feel drowsy again. Then my phone started going haywire, sending repeated messages about resetting to the new time zone, which it never succeeded in doing. Finally, I had to shut it off. When I re-started it, the phone asked for the PIN code. I put in the only one I knew, but I got an error message. I tried again, thinking that I hadn't keyed it carefully enough. I got another error message, and there was only one try left. Apparently the PIN I knew was one specific to my Italian SIM chip, and not to the phone. I got the card for the Hungarian SIM out. There were two PIN numbers. I tried the first, praying that it would work—and it did!

Then the train pulled into the next station—the station where I was supposed to change trains. I gathered my things and started to get off the train. Armed men started to shout at me. They wanted me to get back on the train. Apparently the first border guard was for Hungary, and now we had to go through border control in Romania. I waited and the Romanian border guard re-played the Hungarian guard's grimace, took my passport, and disappeared. This time I started thinking of my partner in ministry. Her passport had been taken by an Alitalia Agent, who lost it. Ten long minutes later, the guard reappeared with my passport and I was allowed to get off the train.

When I went to the ticket window the ticket agent (who

spoke English) said, "I can't sell a ticket because we take only Romanian Lei, and we don't take credit cards." I only had Euros and Hungarian Flotys. "Besides," she continued, "Even if you did have Lei, I can't sell me a ticket." "Why?" I asked. She said, "I can only sell tickets for the Romanian public trains. The train you want is a private train. You have to buy the ticket on the train. And you're going to need Lei."

I thanked her and exited the train station just as it began to drizzle. This little border town was so small it was hardly a town at all. Besides the train station it had a few houses, a bar, and a casino. I had hoped to find a bank, but there was no bank. What was I going to do? There was no place in town to exchange money. I went into the bar, thinking that maybe I could at least get some information.

The bar was small, dark, and shabby, with an uneven wooden floor. It contained three people and two slot machines. The gambling men stopped a moment to look me up and down. Then they returned their attention to their machines. The person not feeding a slot machine was the bartender—a woman. I approached the bar and asked, "Do you speak English?" She shrugged and said, "A little." With gestures and words, I explained that I needed to find a bank, and produced a five Euro note as evidence of my predicament. She frowned in thought, so I defaulted to Italian, saying, "Banca?" Her eyes brightened, "Ah! Banca!" Then she frowned again and said, "No banca here." I said, "Bus?" hopefully. She nodded vigorously and began chattering animatedly with the two men, who had stopped gambling and been listening to the exchange with interest. The three of them argued back and forth a while, then finally the bartender told me in broken English that I should go to the end of the street and take the bus from there to the next town. I said, "Ticket?" She frowned again. I tried Italian: "Biglietto?" The frown remained. From the Budapest subway station I remembered the Hungarian word: "Billet?" She nodded vigorously and produced a bus ticket. Holding up a finger she said, "One Leu." I offered the only thing I had: a one Euro coin. She considered a moment, then made the deal. It was only later that I found out a Leu is worth only one-third of a Euro. I was in no position to haggle, and she knew it.

I stood in front of the casino, where the bartender said the bus would stop. I stood in the cold drizzle feeling foolish. There was no bus stop sign, and town seemed to be deserted. It was definitely one of the dreariest places I've ever been, the dirt street quickly turning to mud. I was glad I brought an umbrella, and I was feeling ready to get out of this town, but where was I going? Had I understood her right? Had she understood me? Which way would the bus come from? Or go? Doubt gnawed at me, but instead of entertaining it, I decided to treat this, too, as an adventure. Here I am, truly going off into the unknown. And even if I'm in a desolate, deserted place, God is always with me, so what's to worry about? If I really believe He's in control, then relax and let Him work it out.

After about ten minutes an elderly woman walked slowly up, an umbrella in one hand and a cane in the other, and took up a place beside me. She asked me something. I smiled and said, "Sorry, I don't speak the language." She nodded, smiling and waving my excuse aside. She said something else to me, but this time obviously not expecting an answer. We exchanged smiles and settled in to wait for the bus together in friendly silence. Frankly, I was glad for the company, and for the assurance that the bus would come.

After about 20 minutes of waiting in the rain, the bus came. It approached from the opposite direction, made a U-turn in the middle of town, and came to the stop in front of us. The old lady got on and tried one seat and then another. I found a seat and took off my backpack. In the seat beside me was a cranky two year old girl. She stopped fussing as soon as she saw PB. She reached out a cautious hand, glancing at me. I smiled and winked at her. She grinned back and grabbed PB by the nose. The whole bus ride she played with PB, and when we got to the next town, I waved goodbye to her. She glanced at her mother, and with mother's encouragement, waved goodbye to me and to PB.

This town is much bigger than the border town, and there were lots of taxis by the bus stop. I asked the first taxi driver, "Do you speak English?" He did! He began chattering away about his brother in Chicago, and I noted that he was wearing a Cubs baseball cap. Finally he asked me where I wanted to go. I explained that I didn't have any Lei, and needed to exchange money. He grinned and loaded my suitcase and backpack into the trunk. He took me about three blocks away, to the Bank of Transylvania (no kidding!). I got some Lei, finally, paid him, and we said goodbye.

I found a sandwich shop and had some lunch. There was a considerable language barrier with people my own age, but many younger people spoke at least some English. Now that I was in a bigger town, it occurred to me to try their train station. I tried asking at the sandwich shop, but got conflicting answers. Without any idea of my way around town, I got another taxi, and asked to go to the train station. This taxi driver also spoke English. He said that the bus was better for going to Biberon (Clara's town), and dropped me off at the bus station. The problem with the bus turned out to be that it wouldn't come until eight tonight. The train from the little border would be there at four. God only knows how late the bus would get into Biberon! I started walking towards what signs pointed to as the center of town, because one way or another, I had several hours to wait.

What do you know! The bus station was only two blocks from the train station. I entered and asked a ticket agent about a train to Biberon. She said that the next train would be in the morning.

At that point, I had tried to call or text Clara, but without success. I decided that it was probably a good idea to stay the night. I found a small B & B, but they didn't have Wi-Fi. So I headed on toward the center of town. As I walked I tried to call Clara just one last time. It rang! But since I was using my Hungarian SIM with very little credit on it, I hung up before she could answer. She called me back, and I told her the situation. She said that if I was OK with staying the night there, she and her husband were coming to town for a funeral, and could just pick me up the next day. Fantastic!

Soon after that, I found a nice little hotel with free Wi-Fi. The cost of the room is €35—not much more than I had paid for the church apartment in Budapest! And she said that she would accept payment in Euros. God is good! But the best part came when I looked in the bathroom: it has a nice, big, deep bathtub! I don't think I have had a good soak in a bath since the last time I was at my house in Texas, about six months ago. After walking much of the afternoon in the chilly rain, a nice warm bath is just what I needed. As I stepped into the tub and relaxed into the warm waters I thought about how good God is to me. God is very, very good!

## Romania

Romanians suffered under one of Communism's cruelest and most oppressive regimes. Christians, in particular, suffered persecution. Now Romania is officially secular, but dominated by the Orthodox Church, in which nominalism, legalism, hypocrisy, and superstition dominate, and other denominations are slandered. It is difficult to legally register denominations or charities. Post-Communist Romania bears the scars of it past in social evils of every kind: substance abuse, prostitution, pornography, human trafficking, entrenched corruption, child abandonment, and one of the highest abortion rates in the world—at three or more abortions to every live birth.

Pray for social and spiritual healing and unity, and an end to institutionalized corruption and injustice. (Operation World, pgs. 700-704.)

## Faith Trip - Days 8 & 9
## Falling In Love with Romania

*If God has called you to be a missionary, don't stoop to be a king.*
*Jordan Groom*

The morning of my first full day in Romania was sunny and warm. After breakfast I continued walking toward the center of town and quickly found 2 things: a Vodafone store where I could buy a Romanian SIM chip for my phone and a McDonalds right next to it—for free Wi-Fi and a coffee. When I had bought the Hungarian SIM back in Budapest they had asked for my passport and all sorts of information, like my mother's last name. The process had taken almost an hour. Here in Romania it took only 10 minutes, and almost half of that was testing to see if a Romanian SIM would work in my phone. They didn't want to know who I was at all! I thought, "No wonder Romania has a problem with organized crime!"

After getting my new SIM I went to McDonalds for coffee and checking e-mail. Then I left McDonalds to go take a look around the city. There was a man sitting just outside on a bench in the sun. He had apparently just finished eating several pieces of chicken (judging from the pile of bones he had left on a paper bag next to him). He was smiling and greeting everyone. He said, "God bless you" to me—in English! His manner was so friendly that I sat on the bench with him and we talked for almost an hour about our loving Lord Jesus. He told me that his name translates as John. He is a sweet, uncomplicated man who loves Jesus with all his heart. We have a lot in common! We laughed a lot, praising God. Then he picked up a sealed plastic bag, and he ripped it open with his teeth and began to drink. It was milk! A liter of milk in a plastic bag. Apparently it is sold that way in Romania. I had never seen milk in a plastic bag before. I laughed when I realized that it was milk because it looked like he was drinking milk right from the cow. John swallowed and laughed, too. We had a wonderful time laughing, talking, and praising Jesus. We were two happy hearts rejoicing together. Naturally, all our laughter caused many people to stare at us as they passed by. That just made us laugh all the more, and John told them that God loves them. Most just shook their heads and walked on by, but who knows? Our joy certainly planted seeds. The Holy Spirit can make those seeds grow and produce fruit, at least that's what I'm praying for. John and I exchanged phone numbers and said a fond good-bye as I caught a tram for the center of town.

I looked for a place to get lunch. I walked past many pizza and falafel places, but I wanted something typically Romanian. Finally, near the Courthouse I found a restaurant specializing in local food. The menu was incomprehensible to me, but the waitress spoke English. I told her that I wanted to eat something typical of the area. She was very pleased, and recommended a vegetable beef soup and pork medallions with beans and red onions. When she brought the soup she also brought a small dish with sour cream and a green chili pepper. I scooped the sour cream into the hot soup and cut up the green pepper into it, too. I had hoped that the pepper would be spicy, but it wasn't. Anyway, everything was really good. The waitress was glad that I had liked the food so much. It was a sincere compliment.

After lunch I walked around the center of town. At the edge

of town many buildings were wrapped in fabric for reconstruction. But the center of town had buildings in bright colors, freshly painted and in good repair. Some of these buildings looked more like giant gingerbread houses than office buildings. There was an air of enchantment, like being in a fairyland, despite the sounds of traffic. I took lots of pictures.

Then I went back to the hotel to wait for Clara. She had told me that the funeral would end at about four. She sent me a text message at 4:45 saying that she was still at the funeral, and would come for me as soon as she could. I told her to take her time. I was reminded of the line by John Milton: "They also serve who only stand and wait." If I had to wait an hour or even two while she comforts the grieving family members, it's no big deal. I can serve both her and them by patiently waiting. Where did I need to run to?

Waiting is an art I learned many years ago. Life is full of situations where you will have to wait. Therefore, I am always prepared to wait. I always have a book to read, paper to write on (just in case inspiration hits!), and/or a crossword or Sudoku book. But most important of all, I've learned to just relax and be in the moment. You'll enjoy life a whole lot more and suffer far less stress if you learn to wait calmly. I was feeling sleepy, so I settled in on the couch in the lobby of the hotel, which was quiet, and took a little nap.

About 45 minutes later Clara came to pick me up. The driver wasn't her husband, but the florist who lives next door to the church. Clara thanked me over and over again for coming to help her. She said that many times people say they will come to help at the church, but then they never do. She was very surprised and pleased that I really did come to help. Her husband, Leo, pastors three satellite churches in addition to the main church of about 300. He leads the youth group, teaches a religion class at the public school, and midweek Bible studies in addition to his pastoring duties for all four churches.

Clara works part time for a private social services company in addition to mothering five children (four of their own and one abandoned to their care), and leads a women's Bible study. Together they also lead a couples group and three weeks of summer Bible camp in the mountains.

She explained all this to me while the driver ran a slalom of enormous potholes at top speed on a narrow two-lane highway. He was simultaneously trying to avoid the oncoming cars that were doing the same thing. There was danger not only of a head-on collision, but hitting a massive, deep pothole at this speed could have been as fatal as hitting a tree. Not being an English-speaker, he was blessedly undistracted by our conversation. I recognized that riding this death slalom was an opportunity to grow my faith. I decided that whether I live or die on this highway, God is in control and would take care of me. After all, "to live is Christ and to die is gain," (Philippians 1:21). Not that I have a death wish or anything like that, but if you really believe that and know your Savior, death is not something to fear.

We came to a place where workers were filling in the potholes, and gratefully enjoyed the fruits of their labors most of the rest of the way to Biberon. Post-Communist Romania has some serious infrastructure problems, which I saw firsthand. Now that the drive was more relaxed I could enjoy the countryside, which was mostly flat. It looked like central Texas, only green. Clara said that all this area is Transylvania. She said that it had once been part of Hungary, and that the people all speak Hungarian in this part of Romania. There was nothing in this pastoral setting that looked at all like the Transylvania that you see in vampire movies, though I tried very hard to see it that way. Clara continued, explaining that the people also speak Romanian, but as a second language. I had noticed that many signs were written in two languages. One language had been completely incomprehensible. The other, while still indecipherable, had certain similarities to Italian. The former had been Hungarian and the latter Romanian.

The trip had taken just under two hours, about half of which had been the death-slalom. The florist pulled into his driveway and helped me get my bags out of the back of his car. The church and Clara's house were both very tidy and pretty. We were met by the younger four children. All but the littlest one were carrying puppies. Clara explained that they breed and sell German Shepherd puppies to make a little extra money.

As she prepared dinner, Clara told me that with the end of Communism all the people who were not working suddenly had to go to work. Those who already had jobs were allowed to keep them, but they earned practically nothing at all. She said that because of this many people had simply left Romania for the west, in search of a better life. The mass-exodus had weakened the fledgling economy so badly that it has never really recovered. A few people have gotten rich in the switch from Communism to Capitalism, but the majority struggle, and many Romanians are very poor indeed. This may explain in part the large number of hopeless homeless I had seen in Budapest.

Clara also told me about her childhood under Communism. Her father was a Baptist pastor and Leo's father was also a pastor in another town. Her father had three churches and his father had eight. Every so often the pastors needed to meet, but the police watched their every move. So they would each bring one of their children, so that it looked like a family outing instead of church business. So, Clara and Leo have known each other since childhood.

Leo went to seminary to become a pastor, too. Because she had seen how difficult the life of a pastor was, Clara never wanted to marry a pastor. When Leo asked her to marry him, she struggled between her affection for him and her unwillingness to be a pastor's wife. She prayed about it, and in the end decided that being obedient was more important than her concerns about the hard life of a pastor's wife. And because she was a pastor's daughter, she knew that she was specially equipped to do the work of a pastor's wife, and could be a real help to Leo in his ministry.

My first day here was mostly spent watching and learning how things work. Soon Clara promised to put me to work, but for the time being, I am learning to fit into a household where only the parents speak English, and only Clara with any fluency.

## Belarus

The 1986 Chernobyl nuclear accident occurred in the

Ukraine, but affected Belarus most severely, and it is still reeling from the economic and health consequences. Two million people fled the contamination which left several thousand dead and dying from radiation-induced cancer. About 20% of the land was affected. Called "Europe's last dictatorship," there is little religious freedom despite a guarantee in the constitution.

Pray for patient, overcoming faith and unity among believers, and for an end to governmental harassment of churches and home groups. (Operation World, pgs. 138-141.)

## Faith Trip - Day 10
## Fitting In with the Family

*Prayer is weakness leaning on omnipotence.*
*W.S. Bowd*

Leo is a man of prayer, and he is training each of his children to pray. At the evening meal (the only meal where everyone is present), each person, no matter how young, takes a turn praying, and at the end of each prayer, everyone says, "AMEN" loudly and emphatically. Hungarian is such a strange and unfamiliar language that it was impossible to predict when AMEN was coming, so my AMEN always lagged behind the rest. Clara explained that breakfast is devotion time, and the children memorize Bible verses. She said that the verse of the day was Ephesians 2:20. I looked it up in English (". . . built on the foundation of the apostles and prophets, with Christ Jesus Himself as the chief cornerstone"). She laughed at my quizzical look and explained that they have been memorizing their way through Ephesians. The children were very good at memorizing, and hardly stumbled at all. The family also sings hymns at the dinner table. I enjoyed our first meals together, and the family fellowship and time of learning. Even if the language barrier prevented me from participating, it didn't prevent enjoyment.

Isaac, age five (the youngest member of the family), was eager to show off (or test) his English. In one of our first encounters, he walked up to me, looked very seriously into my eyes and said, "Dog." To which I replied, "Woof!" He giggled and said, "Sleepy," and I pretended to fall asleep (snoring theatrically). More giggles, then he ran off to play.

When Isaac returned he approached me with the same serious look and recited: "Egy, kettő, három, négy, öt." From the way he said it, I understood them to be numbers, so I counted on my fingers: "Egy, kettő, három, négy, ut." He corrected: "öt." I tried again: "uht." *Öt! Oot!* My English-speaking mouth just can't do those umlauts! It's like the trouble I have with rolling my R's in Italian: even if the brain understands the need to do it, that understanding doesn't make the mouth capable of pronouncing it correctly.

In the morning there was an English lesson for Isaac's kindergarten class. Clara asked me to teach two songs in English (she is their regular English teacher). I had very quickly found out that they already know Head and Shoulders, Knees and Toes—a great one for teaching body parts to children. So I suggested my other standard: The Hokey-Pokey. She knew it and was pleased. And the other? I thought a minute and came up with If You're Happy and You Know It (Clap your Hands). At noon kindergarten let out for the day. I sat in the porch swing watching as the parents came for their children. One little boy came over to me. He said something to me then climbed up and sat with me, swinging and chattering away, not in Hungarian, but probably Romanian. At one point he recited what I thought was probably the days of the week, because they sounded like their Italian counterparts. When his grandfather came to take him home, he said goodbye to me and hurried off.

Afternoon was housecleaning. Clara only allowed me to vacuum my room, but then asked me to take the youngest three children to the piazza in the center of town so she could finish the rest more quickly. There was a large sandbox in the piazza and lots of space for riding bikes and roller-skating. We took a kick scooter and sand pails. The afternoon was sunny and warm. The children raced around the piazza, played in the sand, found an abandoned ball to play with (and ultimately abandoned it, too), and argued over the scooter.

When they appeared to have tired of playing there, I took them for ice cream. They negotiated among themselves over flavors and finally made a choice, saying: "három," which I remembered meant three. What they did was order one flavor (it looked like caramel) for themselves and plain vanilla for me. The only thing left for me to do was to pay. Then each of them said, "Thank you" to me in English. When we got home, they reported the ice cream dutifully to their mother, who offered to pay me back. I told her I would not accept her money because it was a pleasure for me to take them to the piazza, watch them play, and buy them ice cream.

Biberon's central piazza also has an artesian spring. All day long, people line up with empty bottles and fill them at the spring. The water is very good. I volunteered to fill the family's empty water bottles. It was quite an experience, standing in line with the men (seems to be a man's job to get the drinking water) as they smoked and talked and smoked and laughed and smoked and filled their bottles. Standing in line gave me the opportunity to see how it is done: as one bottle fills, you catch a little water in the next bottle and rinse it out so that it's ready for filling. When my turn came, I did just as I had seen the men doing. It's nice that the language barrier can be transcended by watching carefully.

With the little tasks Clara has given me, I have enjoyed myself immensely. I was happy to be able to help out because I recognized immediately that they are real servants of God. Besides eating and sleeping, everything I had seen them do was related to ministry—and come to think of it, so is eating and sleeping because if they didn't take care of their physical needs, they couldn't minister.

It's so true what Jesus said, His burden is light and His yoke is easy. When you're where you're supposed to be, doing what you're supposed to be doing, life becomes a joy and your day is filled with sweet moments of fellowship with Him and with the people around you—transcending language barriers with Look, Listen, Love. I wish that everyone could know the joy and closeness to God and His people like this.

## Belgium

Belgium, "The Crossroads of Western Europe," is a country that is deeply divided between the Flemish-speaking north and the French-speaking south. The growing immigrant population adds another challenging dynamic, with Islam, Hindu, and Sikh as the fastest-growing religions. Though nominally Christian, the vast majority of Belgians consider religion as largely irrelevant.

Pray for the effective use of Christian media (books, TV, radio, and internet) to counter the trend of secularization and situational morality. (Operation World, pgs. 141-145.)

## Faith Trip - Day 11
## More Adventures in School

*The Spirit of Christ is the Spirit of Missions, and the nearer we get to Him the more intensely missionary we must become.*
*Henry Martyn*

I was invited to visit the Elizabeth's school. Elizabeth, the second oldest of Clara and Leo's children, is in middle school. The school rarely gets visitors from outside Romania and even rarer are English speakers. Because of this, I was invited to guest teach three classes, ages 8 - 14. For these older children, I needed a new strategy. They already knew some English, which made things easier. So we played some games: Telephone (also called Gossip), Simon Says, and Hangman. We also did some simple conversation: "Do any of you have a dog? . . . What is your dog's name?" On the walk home from school, I saw several of the students, who greeted me with shy delight. But the most surprising thing of all was that I was asked for my autograph—seven times! Elizabeth was in one of the classes, and she was treated with new respect for having the American as her house guest.

After an early dinner Clara took me and a couple from church to a small town about 20 kilometers away for a Women's Bible Study. The study was at a church she and Leo had planted. The church was mostly finished, but there was still a good deal of construction in progress at the little parsonage next to it. The wife of the couple watched the children while her husband worked on the parsonage.

Clara passed around a small box with little purple flowers and small stones in it. When had I taken the children to the piazza the day before, I had bought wildflowers from a gypsy boy. I had brought them back for Clara and she had put them in a vase in the bathroom. I recognized these flowers as the same ones. I was pleased to see that Clara had found a ministry use for the gypsy boy's flowers. Clara instructed each of us to take either a flower for a praise report or a stone for a prayer request. In our group of seven more flowers than stones were taken. Clara took both a flower and a stone. She said that her prayer request was for wisdom in prioritizing her day every day, and the flower was praise to God for sending me! That felt tremendous! I took a stone and asked for prayers for my friend, Anselmo, who I just heard had been seriously injured in an accident.

This morning Clara and I went to Hargita Christian Centre, a camp in the Carpathian Mountains where in addition to children's' sleepover camps (ages seven and up), they also have Special Needs camps, a Hearing Impaired camp, Visually Impaired Children's camp, Hospice, and Down's Syndrome camp. They also host Women's conferences, and Pastors' and Family Retreats. There is also a Bible School at the camp that trains missionaries and church workers.

One of the missionaries I support in ministry is Juanita, a Bolivian woman who cleans houses for a living and does one-on-one evangelism. One day Juanita asked me if I wanted to go with her to share Jesus with prostitutes. Of course, I said yes. When I asked her where we should meet, she said that she would come to my apartment and we would go together from there. I was shocked. My apartment was in a nice part of Milan, not at all where I thought we would find prostitutes. It was a short walk to our target destination. We only found one prostitute working that night. When Juanita asked if she wanted to hear about Jesus, the girl had eagerly said yes. Then she told the girl briefly the plan of salvation, and followed it up with a tactful "Are you working tonight?" The girl, who said her name was Irina, answered yes, and said that she is from Romania.

On the four-hour-drive to the camp, I remembered Irina and asked Clara about the issue of human trafficking. I had heard that Romania is one of the places where the women enslaved into prostitution come from. She told me about a little girl from Biberon: Christina was a pretty little blonde with blue eyes who her daughter, Elizabeth, knew from school. One day Christina was walking home from school with a friend. Just two blocks from home a man in a car pulled up to the curb and with urgency in his voice said to Christina, "Hurry! Get in the car! Your mother sent me to get you!" She got into the car and has never been seen or heard from again. Christina's friend hadn't thought to notice anything about the man or his car because she had also believed his story. This happened two years ago, when Christina was only ten years old. Most likely Christina has been raped, beaten, and (like Irina) trafficked to a country in Western Europe because she doesn't need a passport to move about within the European Union[1]. I felt like I was

---

[1]  Trafficking is a multi-billion dollar-per-year industry. According to the U.S. Department of Health and Human Services, Texas (my home state)

going to vomit—and it had nothing to do with Clara's driving.

I was relieved when we pulled into the gates at the camp. As beautiful as the setting is at Hargita, Clara had a personal reason for going: her parents live there. As I said, her father had been a pastor during the Communist Era. I was thrilled at the chance to meet her parents. Her father stands straight and tall, sightless eyes gazing at something distant inside himself. Speaking to me in English, his clear, strong voice welcomed me to their home. I could easily imagine that voice preaching stirring sermons, even now in retirement. Her mother is plump and sweet, with eyes that smile in twin upside-down U's, like in Japanese cartoons. Clara's mother doesn't speak English, but every word and gesture was sprinkled so generously with kind intent that her meaning was unmistakably benevolent.

At the camp I also met a remarkable missionary. Her name is Mamie. She has been a missionary in Romania for 35 years. Although she is from the UK, Mamie considers Romania her home. She loves Romania and the Romanian people, and served as a missionary under the brutal Romanian Communist Regime. Mamie is elderly, walks with a cane, and wears a hearing aid. I only got a brief

accounts for 25% of human trafficking in the U.S. For some surprising facts about human trafficking, see:
http://facts.randomhistory.com/human-trafficking-facts.html. Please pray for an end to this diabolical industry, and do whatever you can to stop it in your community.
Please also pray for Christina and the many victims of the human trafficking trade worldwide.

chance to speak with her because she is loved and sought after by young and old alike. Everyone wanted to greet her with a handshake, a hug, and with kisses. I giggled because the casual observer would have thought there was a movie goddess or a rock star in our midst. It was good to see a missionary so loved by the people in the land of her calling. Mamie also lives in retirement most of the year at Hargita Christian Centre.

## Bosnia and Herzegovina

The war of the early 1990's is only the latest in a long history of violence plaguing a region where cultures, languages, and religions intersect. The people groups of Bosnia consist of the Bosniak Muslims, the Orthodox Serbs, the nominally Muslim Romani (Gypsies), and the Muslim Turks. These peoples rarely or reluctantly interact, and there is a constant struggle with poverty, organized crime, and pessimism (which has caused 60% of the youth to want to leave the country).

Pray for unity among believers so that they may share the hope of Jesus Christ with their fellow Bosnians. (Operation World, pgs. 157-159.)

## Faith Trip - Day 12
## Gypsies

*The weakness of much current mission work is that we betray the sense that what is yet to be done is greater than what Christ has already done. The world's gravest need is less than Christ's great victory.*
*P.T. Forsyth*

There are many things Clara told me about Romania that simply astonished me. On the way home from Hargita, I asked about the gypsies. I was curious because many of Italy's gypsies come from Romania. People I know who work with the gypsies call them by their proper name, Roma or Romani, because the label "gypsy" is considered derogatory. The name Roma is from their origins in India, and means "a man who makes his living singing," though few do that now.

Clara said that in Romania they are just called gypsies. She said that there are two types of gypsies in Romania. One type is very visible because the women wear long, brightly colored skirts and scarfs and the men wear big hats, and large mustaches. These, she told me, are businessmen gypsies. The men work, but never in the employ of others. They tend to be independent businessmen who do a large variety of repair work or independent sales, selling all sorts of goods. They work off the books and do not report their income or pay taxes. I don't know how they manage to get away with this. Perhaps they have a deal with the government, or more likely, they move on before the authorities can catch up with them. On the drive back to

Biberon she showed me a gypsy mansion, saying that some gypsies even become rich from their businesses. She said that she and Leo planted a gypsy church with the businessmen gypsies. One rich gypsy family invited them to their mansion, taking them all through the house, which was lavishly furnished. But she said that they don't live in their mansion. They built a tiny house in the back yard where twelve of them live together in two rooms. She said that they prefer living all together, and that the mansion was strictly for show.

The other type of gypsies don't work, but beg or pick flowers to sell. These are nomadic gypsies—and nomadic even in their relationships because they tend to couple and uncouple. They move on, leaving their children either with a former partner or just abandoning them to the streets.

At a gas station on the way, we saw a gypsy girl, about seven years old, begging in tears. The desperation on her face was heartbreakingly obvious. If she doesn't bring back an acceptable amount of money, she will be beaten—and that's if she hasn't already been abandoned to the streets. The Romanian government has tried to help these poorest of children by making it profitable to the parents to keep their children in school. But even receiving money from the government doesn't appear to be enough of an incentive because the children's attendance is spotty at best.

The plight of gypsy children is the worst childhood possible—if you can even call that existence a childhood. Among both types of gypsies it is typical for the children of both sexes to be passed among the adults as sex toys. The nomadic gypsy children are also expected to sell flowers and/or beg to bring in money. Sometimes a parent will cut off their child's legs or feet, or break their bones and set them so that they grow together crooked. The deformed child is thought to earn more money than a healthy child. The thought of a parent deliberately crippling a healthy child nauseated me.

Clara continued to say that some children are sent out to work as prostitutes. Others are sold into slavery, sold to the black market for their organs, or simply abandoned. A missionary couple I know who work with gypsies in Italy had explained gypsy cultural values to me. In a nutshell, gypsy values are all about the family: if this helps the family (especially financially), then it's a good thing. So sending your daughter out as a prostitute is a good thing because she will bring back money for the family. Paying taxes, on the other hand, is a bad thing because it takes money away from the family. Clara confirmed that this is also her understanding of gypsy culture.

Clara told me the good news is that gypsies who have accepted Christ stop doing these things and living this way. This is a tremendous work of God for these people to give up their whole culture. Only the Holy Spirit living within them can bring about this kind of transformation.

Praise God for those who work with the gypsies, as it is work that requires a lot of patient endurance. Please pray for the gypsy people, and especially for their children. And also pray for those who work with the gypsies. Although the work is very hard and they see a lot of suffering, they do see fruit and lives changed. Every time European gypsies are mentioned in Operation World, they are noted as being the people group that is most open to the Gospel, and ironically one of the universally least-reached throughout Europe.

## Bulgaria

Bulgaria straddles the Balkan, Slavic, and Turkish worlds. This has caused trouble for centuries, and Bulgaria's ethnic minorities have suffered severely at the hands of the Bulgarian majority. Discrimination continues for the Rumelian Turks, the Romani (Gypsies), the Millet (Turkish-speaking Gypsies), and Bulgarian-speaking Muslims. Additional trouble exists in the form of corruption, organized crime, poverty, divorce, and abortion. Bulgaria has more abortions than live births.

Pray for an end to the cycle of trouble, for unity among believers and open, receptive hearts among those who need to find hope. (Operation World, pgs. 173-176.)

## Faith Trip - Day 13
## Battling Superstition

*You do not test the resources of God until you attempt the impossible.*
*F.B. Meyer*

Another conversation Clara and I had is about is the Romanian Orthodox church (though after what she told me, I hesitate to call it a church). Clara's father was a Baptist pastor, and so was Leo's father. Therefore, neither of them has had a great deal of contact within the Romanian Orthodox church. The Romanian Orthodox church was the only "legal" church under communism.

Clara told me about an Orthodox funeral she attended. She said that there was no mention of Jesus and no reading from the Bible, there wasn't even a Bible in sight. She said that the priest lit incense and waved the censer over each person in attendance at the funeral. This was done to discover who had put a curse on the deceased to cause his death.

She explained that people in the Romanian Orthodox church pay their priests for blessings and pay the priests to curse their enemies. And she said that frequently people die after being cursed by the priest! She said that if they fail to pay the priest or fail to pay him enough money, he will curse them, and they may die, too. I said, "This sounds more like Shamanism than Christianity," and Clara agreed.

She went on to say that during the funeral, which lasted

three hours, each person in attendance was required to eat a bite of food at the head of the coffin. Again, this was done to discover who had cursed the deceased and thus caused his death. This made Clara feel nauseated, and she left the funeral, rather than participate in this un-Christian ritual. She said that it was days before she felt a return to normalcy after the funeral.

I looked for information on the internet about the Romanian Orthodox church, but found nothing to support what Clara said. Nevertheless I believe her. One thing I did note was that the Romanian Orthodox church was controlled through "special delegates" during the Communist period. And that the actions of both laity and clergy, ranged broadly from "opposition to the regime and martyrdom," to "silent consent or collaboration," according to Wikipedia. And the church's shield shows little that is even remotely Christian.

Speaking of the Communist era, there are two things in the pastoral countryside that remain to this day from the Communist era: one is the oil pipeline and the other is the presence of enormous chimneys resembling the cooling towers for nuclear reactors.

Being Texan, I am accustomed to the sight of the oil-pumpers that look like giant, rocking crickets. So when I saw one by the highway, I asked Clara about it. She confirmed that it was pumping oil, but she said that all the oil in Romania belongs to Russia. I wondered how on earth the Russians could get away with just taking the Romanian's most precious natural resource. I suppose the obvious answer is that they drilled and pumped the oil, and therefore have the rights to the profits from it, but it hardly seems fair. The majority of Romanian oil is piped away to other countries in the west. The pipeline is visible all across the landscape.

The enormous chimneys were not nuclear reactor cooling towers, as I had guessed, but giant boilers. The Communists built these giant boilers to give heat (in the form of hot water) to all the houses in the neighborhood, community, or village. This seemingly benevolent act had a sinister purpose. If people complained or failed to comply (even a single individual), the whole neighborhood was punished by being deprived of heat. Most of the boilers have been torn down and replaced with by independent heating. Communism has certainly left its mark on the Romanian people, and not only on the countryside.

## Croatia

Historic hatred between the Croats, Serbs, and Bosnians was one of the causes of the Balkan wars of the 1990's, and continues to hamper progress and stifle spiritual renewal. Of particular concern are young the people of Croatia, who exhibit hopelessness, functional godlessness, and little confidence in the future due to high unemployment. Drug use among teens is 80%.

Pray for an end to racial/religious hatred and for unity and creativity among believers in sharing the love of Jesus. (Operation World, pgs. 289-291.)

## Faith Trip - Days 14, 15, & 16
## Hero of the Day!

*All God's giants are weak men who did great things for*
*God because they reckoned that God was with them.*
*Hudson Taylor*

Clara and Leo went to host a marriage weekend retreat at
Hargita Christian Camp. The flower man next door (who
had driven the death-slalom highway) loaded them up with
flowers to decorate the meeting room. I had been
introduced to the flower man, but his name was so difficult
to pronounce that it just never stuck with me. They left me
in charge of the two oldest children, Benjamin (age
fourteen) and Elizabeth (twelve), and had taken the
youngest, Isaac (five) and Ruth (eight, their ward).
Amanda (nine) had gone to spend the weekend at a friend's
house.

Both Benjamin and Elizabeth speak a little English, but at
the first unknown word from me, Benjamin went to the
kitchen laptop computer and consulted Google Translate. I
laughed and brought my netbook into the kitchen. We had
a very funny and strange conversation through Google
Translate.

Here's the thing: Google Translate is not to be trusted. It
translates each word without regard to the context. So if a
word has more than one meaning, Google Translate will
pick one of the possible meanings regardless of the
context. For example, a friend in Italy was teasing me
about Boo-Boo, my cat. He told me: "Sei antipatica come il

tuo gatto." Then he put that sentence into Google Translate and it came out: "Six nasty like your cat." He shook his head, saying, "Why six?" Then we both understood: Google Translate had translated the Italian verb "sei" (second person, singular, familiar) as the number six because they are spelled exactly alike. The moral of the story is: if it's important to get the meaning right, always double check Google Translate—and with a human whenever possible. But the results can be pretty funny!

Things had been really quiet, with the only notable event in the last couple of days being that I bought a train ticket for an overnight train to Bucharest for my return to Italy. Then just hours after Clara and Leo had left, I was locking the door behind me when **THUP!** The key broke off in the lock. I couldn't believe it! The door was locked shut with no way to open it, and Benjamin was inside the house. I called up to him and tried to explain the problem, showing him the stub of the key. He asked me to bring the ladder to the window so he could get out. While he was still in the house, Benjamin tried to call his dad, but got no answer. He climbed out the window, and he went next door to ask the flower man for help, but the flower man was out. In the meantime Leo called Benjamin back, and told him to call the locksmith (I had been telling him that all along, but without Google Translate he hadn't understood). The locksmith didn't answer the phone so Benjamin took his bike and went to the locksmith's office. He returned five minutes later, saying that the locksmith is in the hospital, and the office is closed.

After another call to his dad, Benjamin went into the

basement (a daylight basement) and came out with a hammer and a screwdriver. He inserted the point of the screwdriver between the doors near the top and hammered until the fastener came loose and he was able to open both doors. Then he started taking the lock apart. Just then the flower man showed up. The two of them got the lock part to slide out and Benjamin took it to the hardware store, along with the emergency money his parents had left.

Flower man went back home, and I sat there by the door, feeling like the biggest dope that ever lived. However, I had just received a prophetic Word that morning, saying that I was not to worry, but to really give thanks in all circumstances and to let God work. So I let go of that emotion, and as it slowly slid away, I started thanking God with all the enthusiasm I could muster. All this sounds easy, but took a good deal of effort at first. As soon as I began thanking God, I realized that the only thing that had been causing me to worry was my pride. And on the heels of that realization came another: that this had happened in order to help me let go of my pride. With those two realizations I was able to thank God with genuine enthusiasm for having broken the key in the lock because ultimately it was for my good! God really does work all things for the good of those who love Him (Romans 8:28). Knowing that changed my whole outlook. Knowing that has made "giving thanks to God the Father for everything" (Ephesians 5:20) so much easier. It has also revealed worry for what it really is: a ridiculous waste of energy that is often fueled by wrong thinking.

Hallelujah! Thank You, Lord, that I broke the key in the

lock! Thank You for whatever Clara and Leo think of me now! Thank You for helping me let go of my stupid pride! Hallelujah! God, You are good!

Benjamin came back with all the money and a new lock (hardware guy is in the church and said he would settle up with Leo later). He installed the new lock with some difficulty, but finally he got it in and got the bolt to slide open again. Then he re-fastened the other side of the door. I was relieved to finally have the lock fixed. I'm still feeling pretty stupid, but not worried about it. Then I realized another important reason to thank God for this incident: it gave Benjamin the opportunity to handle a problem and fix it responsibly—empowering his young manhood. God is good!

## Cyprus

Cyprus is essentially two countries, though only the Republic of Cyprus (in the southern two-thirds of the island) is recognized. The Turkish Republic of Northern Cyprus has a population that is almost entirely Muslim. Due to economic isolation, poverty and high unemployment makes the TRNC heavily dependent upon Turkish subsidies and trade. Cyprus is largely non-practicing Orthodox, but serves as a major base for several Christian organizations: missions groups, Bible and Christian literature printing, SAT-7 (Christian satellite TV broadcasting), and Christian Radio stations.

Pray for fruit from these ministries, and for hearts open and ready to receive God's Word. (Operation World, pgs. 295-298.)

## Faith Trip - Day 17
## My Turn to be the Hero!

*Prayer succeeds when all else fails. Prayer has won great victories and has rescued, with notable triumph, God's saints when every other hope is gone.*
*E.M. Bounds*

Clara and Leo came back from their weekend couples retreat looking rested and very happy. Clara said that there were over 70 couples, which is a huge response for Romania. She brought greetings from her parents, who told her to thank me for watching the children. She said that usually she has to stay home while Leo conducts the couples weekend alone. To me it seemed such a simple thing, but for her it was a big thing. I'm just happy to be where God can use me to bless His people. Leo and Clara work tirelessly all day, every day to minister to their flock. Like I said, everything they do is ministry-related.

They returned half an hour before the Sunday evening service, and immediately began to get ready to go to church. Leo gave the sermon, even though he had been away all weekend leading a couples retreat, and had just driven four and a half hours. He didn't look tired, which had to be a sign of power from the Lord God, Himself.

When the service was over many people left, but most stayed. Clara explained that they were having a members meeting. Since it was about seven in the evening, I asked if I could help by getting dinner prepared. She gave me a huge smile and thanked me for thinking of it. So I returned to the house and made spaghetti with a tomato and pepper sauce, which everybody seemed to like (everybody took seconds). Again, such a small thing can be a big help.

I have come to realize more and more that the skills learned in my previous life as a housewife and mother have seamlessly translated into ministry to missionaries and local churches. Nothing is wasted in God's economy.

After dinner I packed my bags for the overnight train to Bucharest. I had to go back to Italy to pick up my Permit to Stay. Since the Permit had already been approved, I didn't expect any problems, but prayer never hurts. Leo and Clara and all the children prayed for my safe travel and trouble-free time getting my Permit. Then Leo drove me to the train station. Thanks to God who makes the little things count big-time!

## Czech Republic

Freedom for the Czechs has translated into a "free-for-all" with unfortunate emphasis on hedonistic materialism, and a descent into crime, sexual immorality, and substance abuse. Depression and suicide are more prevalent now than in Communist times. The Catholic Church has been in "free-fall," losing both numbers and influence.

Pray for revival that will reverse these sad trends and bring hope to the Czech people. (Operation World, pgs. 298-300.)

## Faith Trip - Day 18
## The Romanian Runaround

*Do not pray for easier lives; pray to be stronger men. Do not pray for tasks equal to your powers; pray for powers equal to your tasks. Then, the doing of your work shall be no miracle, but you shall be a miracle.*
*Bishop Phillips Brooks*

I took the overnight train to Bucharest and woke up in the ugliest city I've ever seen. To be fair, even beautiful cities are ugly in the area of the train station. Since I had all morning to look around I wanted to buy my bus ticket to the airport first so that I could explore in a more relaxed way.

Getting from the train station to the airport would turn out not to be as simple as it would seem. There is no train that goes to Baneasa Airport, so I needed to get a bus, but the bus wasn't where the English-speaking train ticket agent said it would be. A helpful lady told me where to find the bus, and which bus to take. Since she didn't speak English, it's really amazing that she was able to make me understand that I needed to take bus number 205. She didn't know how to tell me where to buy bus tickets so I went back to the train ticket agent to ask. Again the ticket agent gave me bad information, but in looking for an open door where she had told me to go, a helpful man in a van took my bag and led me to ticket line. He also didn't speak English, but I was able to make him understand that the problem was that I had no ticket.

Ugly city (thanks, no doubt, to its Communist dictators and Romania's crumbling infrastructure), but populated by beautiful, helpful, kind people—God bless the Romanian people! I pray for more missionaries to share the Good News about Jesus with the Romanian people. God bless the ticket agent who gave me bad directions, too. I know she didn't deliberately send me in the wrong direction, and it didn't do me any harm, either. In fact, it allowed me to see just how kind the Romanian people are with strangers who don't speak the language.

I finally got my bus ticket and found out what time I needed to catch the bus. I began walking away from the train station to explore as much of the city as I could. Unfortunately, I didn't get very far because the thing I never did locate was a baggage deposit at the train station, so I had to bring my suitcase and backpack with me. What I saw on my brief walk was more of Romania's crumbling infrastructure, and more roadwork in progress. The bone-jarring jackhammers beat out a rhythm that set my nerves on edge. Several blocks from the train station, and Bucharest was as ugly as ever. It didn't seem like it was worth the effort, so I headed back to the train station.

At about noon I took the bus to the airport. From the bus I did see a prettier side of Bucharest. The bus took a slow turn on a big roundabout with an arch in the middle. I wasn't able to get a good picture of the arch because the day had turned cloudy and drizzly, but I was glad that Bucharest is not the ugly city it first appeared to be.

I got off the bus at the airport stop, but nothing looked like an airport in any direction. None of the other passengers had baggage, so I crossed the street, following the majority. They quickly dispersed. I entered an office building, partly because it had begun to rain in earnest. I asked the receptionist where the airport was. Thankfully, she spoke some English. She pointed kitty-corner across the street, which still didn't look even remotely like an airport. How can a city hide a big thing like an airport? By then it had started to rain very hard, and I didn't have an umbrella with me. What I did have was time, so I decided to wait until the rain let up, and about ten minutes later it did. So just to clarify, I asked the receptionist: "It's across this street and also that one?" and she said yes. So in faith I crossed both streets and started walking in the most promising direction. Soon I saw a building with a Romanian flag on it that appeared to be the airport authority office building, though the sign was unintelligible. Continuing, I finally found the airport, which is tiny and looks like a spaceship.

There were three gates, and all three had flights departing at the same time. That means that there was a crush of people at security, and the waiting area was standing room only for the two hours leading up to departure time. Otherwise, I had an uneventful flight back to Milan. Travel is exhausting, but God is good!

## Denmark (and Faeroe Islands)

Both Denmark and the self-governing Faeroe Islands have complete freedom of religion, with the Lutheran Church recognized as the national church and supported by taxes. After the "cartoon riots" of 2006, Denmark has had to confront the issues of free speech, religious sensitivity, and intercommunity relations.

Pray for traditionalism, ritualism, and nominalism to transform into genuine faith in Jesus Christ, and for sensitivity in dealing with Muslims. (Operation World, pgs. 302-303; 331-332.)

## Faith Trip - Day 19
## Containing My Joy in Bunnyland!

*Your righteousness is like the mighty mountains, your
justice like the great deep. O Lord, you preserve both man
and beast.*
*Psalm 36:6*

I spent the night with Pina and Luigi in Milan and went to
pick up my Permit to Stay. I was going to go straight to the
train station from the *Questura* (the police station), to catch
a train to Florence. I didn't want to carry all my
documentation with me—I hadn't thought I would need it,
since I was only picking up the Permit. I had only brought
the appointment paper with me. Since all the paperwork
had been completed, and the Permit granted, logically, the
appointment paper and my old Permit should have been
everything necessary.

However, I was dealing with the Italian government, so
logic has very little to do with anything. What they asked
for is the receipt from the Post Office from when I had
made the appointment to apply for my Permit. I hadn't
brought it with me, because obviously I had made the
appointment—the Permit had been granted! The illogic
and inefficiency of the Italian government can drive you
crazy if you don't just let it go! They told me to come back
with the receipt the following week. I didn't allow myself
to sink into disappointment, but chose to see this as a
blessing because it gave me time to go to the bank before
catching the train.

I needed to go to the bank to transfer funds into my checking account because I'm buying a motor home. It sounds crazy, but the idea of living in a motor home had been buzzing around in my head for about three years. In the previous two weeks, the idea has been so insistent that I finally had to ask God for some clarity. I said, "Lord, if this is what You want me to do, then I need for You to put the motor home right in front of me, already done." Talk about a fleece! Well, that's exactly what happened. Bob, a missionary friend, contacted me with a motor home already picked out, insurance issues figured out, etc. He wanted to see if I would be interested in time-sharing a motor home. So, the plan was that while in Italy, I would go south and buy the motor home.

But first I wanted to spend a few days in Florence, visiting my son, Kevin, who is spending his summer here. While in Florence I will be staying with *Gesù È La Risposta* (Jesus is the Answer) mission organization. They are camped outside the city in a bunch of containers and old campers. I had contacted them out of necessity for a place to stay, for mission purposes of encouraging them, and a healthy dose of curiosity about their set up. The containers are much nicer than they sound, having been completely outfitted as living quarters. And the folks there are a very welcoming group of people, very committed to sharing the love of Jesus.

My ministry partner and I had visited some small towns in Abruzzo the week before Easter. At that time we realized that there was nobody going into the small towns in Italy to speak to the people about Jesus. But Gesù È La Risposta is going into the small towns. To my knowledge they're the only ones going into the small towns in Italy.

As I was shown around the camp, I saw dozens and dozens of bunnies: outside the main meeting tent, beside the kitchen container, along the path to the showers, etc. Since bunnies are nocturnal, it made me wonder just how many there were. It had to be in the hundreds, if I was seeing this many in the daytime. "Welcome to Bunnytown!" I thought, smiling to myself.

### Finland

Humanism, secularism, and materialism are strong in Finland. The national Lutheran Church has a tradition of evangelism, but faces the challenge of liberalism, which attempts to restrict evangelical preaching and teaching. There is also a vacuum of young leadership created by the aging and often out-of-touch church population. Liberal and conservative elements within the Church have had a divisive effect, creating new denominations. Many believers "church-hop," failing to commit, causing disillusioned believers to simply stay away.

Pray for vital, young leadership that will revitalize the national church, and for revival and unity throughout all the churches of Finland. (Operation World, pgs. 337-339.)

## Faith Trip - Day 20
## The Price Paid

*A man is what he is on his knees—nothing more and nothing less.*
*Robert Murray McCheyne*

I didn't get to know the team at the Gesù È La Risposta container camp as well as I would have liked to, but I know that sometime I will catch up with them again for a visit focused more on them. They blessed me tremendously by giving me a place to stay while I was visiting my son, Kevin, in Florence. For that I am truly grateful to them.

I had a really nice visit with Kevin. We had gone to a pizzeria and watched Italy beat Estonia on TV, and visited some of our favorite places in Florence.

It was bittersweet, visiting with him because it made me more aware of how alone I am. Kevin had somehow gotten the idea that my return to Italy was an attempt to run away from my problems back in the US. I said, "What problems?" He said, "Well, you know, after the divorce and all." I explained that I wasn't running from problems, but running toward a mission, a ministry that is important. I hear the ticking of the world's clock, and I know that the time is short.

Being so badly misunderstood by my own son made me feel lonely, and I told him so. Most of the time it doesn't bother me to be alone because I stay busy, traveling, meeting people, doing things, reading, writing, etc. But in the odd moments a feeling of loneliness sometimes catches me by surprise. I think my marriage actually trained me to be happy alone. My ex had been out of the house 12 hours every day, and had traveled frequently for business, so I was alone much of the time during my marriage. I had spent many days exploring Milan and beyond —independent even while tied by marriage and family responsibilities to my home each evening. Divorce just expanded the boundaries of my independence. I value my independence. In fact, I don't know anybody who appreciates independence more than I do. But independence does have its price.

As I explained all this to him, Kevin understood, relieved, but saddened by my loneliness. I said, "Hey, I don't dwell on it, so don't you, either." And with that, he walked me to the train station and on to the next adventure. My life is too full of good moments to waste time crying over the few sad ones.

I caught a train to Monte Pannolini, where I would be staying with Bob and Jill and their family. They are a young couple with three active little boys. Bob and Jill work with young people and are getting ready to build a parkour environment[2] and family vacation retreat. I had never heard of parkour before meeting them. It's looks fun, but is definitely a young person's sport. These days I don't go down stairs without holding onto the railing.

---

[2]  If you've ever seen a Jackie Chan movie, where he runs up walls and jumps off rooftops (Rumble in the Bronx is a good example), that is parkour. It is using the urban environment as your gym.

Nevertheless, I can appreciate how much fun it must be when you're young, and your equilibrium, eyesight, and joints are all functioning properly. I look forward to seeing their project when it has been built and is open for business.

After that I'll go back to Milan and get my Permit to Stay (taking the Post Office receipt this time!). I would really like to go back to Romania by way of Bulgaria. I have a missionary to meet with in Bulgaria, and another container team in Romania. But those plans still need to take better shape. As always, God is good!

## Estonia

Foreign investment and sustained economic growth has made Estonia one of the most successful post-Soviet economies. Poverty remains, but with overall wealth there is materialism and a crisis of values. Religious freedom is an open door to Christian ministry, but also to marginal sects. Mormons have more missionaries in Estonia than any Christian organization. Estonians are increasingly drawn to pre-Christian pagan religions. Genuine faith is rare in Estonia. There is a need for outreach to Tatar Muslims, Jews, and other growing minority groups in Estonia.

Pray for unity within the Body of Christ, and for revival that will bring genuine faith. (Operation World, pgs. 325-327.)

## Faith Trip - Days 21 & 22
## Camper!—Well, Almost!

*I will instruct you and teach you in the way you should go;*
*I will counsel you and watch over you.*
*Psalm 32:8*

Yesterday I posted about loneliness on my blog. It got a huge response from readers. It seems that loneliness is a theme that resonates with a lot of people. While I am alone most of the time, I don't *feel* lonely. I have spent much of my life in solitude. I enjoy my life, and cherish solitude. I can't always collect my thoughts when I'm surrounded by people who are constantly engaging me in conversation. That's not to say that I want to be a hermit, either. Solitude is a thing to be used and enjoyed, not to avoid. It's just that solitude does sometimes have the negative effect of loneliness. However, just to reiterate, what caused the feeling of loneliness that I mentioned yesterday wasn't "being alone." Instead it had been caused by the realization that I my son had misunderstood me. He thought that I had returned to live in Europe because I was running away from "problems" in the US, and running away from the family.

Nothing could be farther from the truth! I came to Europe in answer to the call of the God I love. I am living a life full of fun and adventure. This Faith Trip is exciting for me. I am living my dream come true—and never more so than right here and now in this Faith Trip.  Following wherever God leads me, meeting the people He has me meet, maybe it doesn't interest everybody, but for me this is more thrilling than a rollercoaster ride. And if everyone would let go of whatever is holding them back, and let God truly lead, they would find their own dream come true, their own adventure. He made each of us different, so my dream isn't necessarily anyone else's dream. I had explained all this to Kevin, and he understood: I wasn't running away from anything. I was running *to* my life.

I rented a car at the train station and Bob, his youngest son, Isaiah, and I went to L'Aquila look at the motor home. Bob told me that he wasn't sure Isaiah would want to come because sometimes, at age two and a half, he can be quite stubborn and vocal about it if he doesn't get his way. But he said that Isaiah had woken up this morning and the first words out of his mouth were, "I want to go to L'Aquila." Bob hadn't even mentioned the possibility to him! Praise God!

I was not disappointed when I saw the camper. It's bigger inside than I had hoped—it's actually spacious! And it's smaller on the outside than I had feared. I had been concerned about being able to drive it and park it and back it up, but it's only a little bigger than my brother's big ol' Ford pickup truck, which I've driven many times. And the camper is really cute. I am very happy with it.

However, when it came time to sign the papers, my expired Permit to Stay was a problem, after all. But this is a good thing, too. The dealer isn't just taking my money, he wants to do things right. And since he's also giving me a guarantee, that tells me that should something go wrong with the camper, I can bring it back and he'll make it right.

86

It amounted to nothing more than an inconvenience because it meant that I would have to go back to Milan to pick up my Permit before I could legally buy the camper. G.K. Chesterton said: "An inconvenience is only an adventure wrongly considered; an adventure is an inconvenience rightly considered." It's all about attitude, right?

It was late in the day when I left Monte Pannolini. I had been in touch with Carla, one of the team of people praying for me. She had invited me to come stay with her, and since she lived in a town about halfway between Monte Pannolini and Milan, I accepted. Carla and I had only known each other on Facebook, but her messages to me told me that she is someone with a quirky sense of humor and deep faith in God. In other words, someone like me. I had hoped to be able to meet her, and here was my opportunity. So I called the number she had given me and made arrangements to stay at her house. I wasn't disappointed. I spent the night at her house, went to Milan, to pick up my Permit, and returned to spend tonight with her again on the way back.

And I did get my Permit, and will return to Monte Pannolini tomorrow to finalize the camper deal. God is good, and He's always in control!

# France

As with many European countries, France has problems with an aging native citizenry and young, breeding immigrant population. The country is fiercely secular, which has caused some problems with the large, mostly Muslim immigrant population. There are nearly 50 million French people who have no real link with a Christian church, about 35,000 rural communities and small towns have no evangelical church presence—particular need is in the Loire Valley, Brittany, Picardy, and Centre regions, and among the Basques and on the island of Corsica.

Pray to the Lord of the Harvest to send workers into these regions, and for hearts open and ready to receive the Good News. (Operation World, pgs. 340-345.)

## Faith Trip - Day 23
## Hurry up & Wait!

*Be still before the Lord and wait patiently for Him . . .*
*Psalm 37:7a*

Gazing out the window . . . drumming my fingers . . .
picking up a book to read, and putting it down again . . .
*sigh* . . . waiting is boring! I'm embarrassed at how much
I've bragged about being so good at waiting. I'm good at
waiting for several hours, but waiting several days is
another thing. With each passing day, the prospect of
returning to Romania for this work with the gypsies grows
more and more remote. That's where my heart is now. Or
in California with my other son, Josh, as he waits for the
birth. I feel like an insect pinned to a child's poster
board—I'm stuck here!

Buying a camper has proven to be both more easy and
more complicated than I had thought. Since I'm buying
from a dealer, he has been very helpful, knowing how to
fill out all the paperwork, and having connections for
camper insurance at reduced rates.

But since I'm buying in Italy, buying a camper is not
something that happens fast because, well, it's Italy. But
that's not a bad thing, either. My problem is that, being
American, I expect things to go faster than they do here.
That's something that simply doesn't happen, and I really
just need to get over it.

I've made a down-payment, so the camper went to the

garage to be inspected. This is something I thought would be fairly fast, one day at most. Even if there are a lot of people ahead of me, getting my car inspected never takes longer than a day. But this is not a car, it's a camper. They have to inspect all sorts of things like the gas connection for the stove, the plumbing and holding tanks, electrical connections, and look for leaks in the doors, windows, and roof. All this is in addition to the expected inspection of the motor and other "vehicle" parts. So inspection will take a minimum of three days—once it reaches the front of the line. With all the other campers also being inspected at the same time, it could take a week.

Meanwhile I'll have to just wait around for another week or so. There are a few missionaries to meet with in the area, so ministry will continue moving forward. There is also the sea, and I don't think it would be a bad thing to go walk by the sea and dip my toes in the water from time to time while I wait. What else have I got to do?

Teach me, Lord, how to wait! If You want me to go back to Romania, You'll have to speed this process up. If not, what is it that You want me to do next? I feel like I'm going nuts!

## Greece

The Greek economy is of grave concern, not only within the country, but for all the rest of the European Union. Protests and riots are increasingly common and often violent. Fewer than 3% of the population regularly attend church. Most Greeks are ignorant of the gospel message, and are unreceptive to any non-Orthodox witness. Among unreached areas: the 150 islands, university students, Albanians (Greece's largest ethnic minority), immigrant communities, indigenous ethnic minorities in the north, the 200,000 drug addicts, and the 10,000 prostitutes (many of whom were trafficked in from other countries.

Pray for unity in the Spirit, wisdom in outreach, courage to witness, and open, receptive heart. (Operation World, pgs. 370-373.)

## Faith Trip - Day 24
## The Inner Voyage

*What shall we say, then? Shall we go on sinning so that grace may increase? By no means! We died to sin; how can we live in it any longer?*
*Romans 6:1-2*

I had thought that I had made a lot of progress in my spiritual walk—and I think I have made some—but God revealed to me that I'm not finished yet. I was returning the rental car, and first I couldn't find the right street, then I couldn't find the car rental agency, then I couldn't find a parking place. I have mostly conquered fear and worry, but I have always had a problem with frustration. The more I drove around, searching in the heavy morning traffic, and the closer the deadline approached for returning the car, the more frustrated I became. When I heard the word "dammit" pop out of my mouth, I knew I had stopped trusting God. I took a deep breath and went back to the principle of Look, Listen, Love. Soon, I found my way (in both senses!).

When I came back to the house, I read: "The cause of the weakness of your Christian life is that you want to work it out partly, and to let God help you. And that cannot be. You must come to be utterly helpless, to let God work, and God will work gloriously[3]." I know that it's true, and this is from a great book I'm reading called <u>Absolute Surrender</u>.

---

[3] Murray, Andrew (2004). Absolute Surrender (Optimized for Kindle) (Kindle Locations 718-719). Unknown. Kindle Edition.

If we really want to grow spiritually, we've got to be ready to surrender it all to Him.

In fact, my pastor back in Texas asked us one Sunday morning, "Do you want more from God?" My answer to that question was: "YES, I want *everything* God has for me!" And I understood that if I want more from God, I have to be willing to surrender it all to Him. On first instinct, I wanted to hold tightly to all my stuff, but once I really thought about it, I realized that everything in my life came to me from God in the first place. He didn't hold any good things back from me, why would I hold anything back from Him? It was that first moment of true surrender that put my life as a missionary into motion. I've never regretted it.

Later I was rushing down the street and fell flat on my face. I wasn't badly hurt, just bruised my left knee. I really need to slow down. This is the second time I've literally fallen on my face in the last couple of months.

I might need to switch back to single-vision lenses, too! Bifocals are convenient for reading, but being near-sighted, they render everything from the waist down to a watery blur.

I had been rushing down the street, trying to help Bob and Jill. They are getting ready to go on an extended trip through Europe, and I will be house-sitting for them until Jill's parents come Sunday evening. So Bob, Jill, and I were rushing around, trying to get the last few things done before they leave town in the camper (which we are time-sharing).

Again, I was able to bless God's people by watching their kids and cooking meals. Like I noted with Clara and her family, missionary support sometimes looks a lot like what I did as a housewife and mother. Caring for a family (yours or the family of someone you love) is important work, even if it will never make you rich. God will reward you in some surprising ways. He certainly did me!

So today's lesson for me was to stop rushing around, remember to Look, Listen, Love, and don't let frustration take over. I've got to let God be God, and just thankfully live my life, enjoying the blessings of the present moment. Sometimes growth comes with bruises, but God is always good!

## Iceland

Iceland has one of the highest standards of living in the world. The highest rate of immigration in Europe threatens traditional Icelandic life. The majority of Icelanders are Christian, but only nominally.

Pray for outreach initiatives to reach people even in remote areas: Bibles in Icelandic, including the 2007 release of the 100-Minute Bible, and Christian radio (also via the internet). (Operation World, pgs. 404-405.)

## Faith Trip - Day 25
## A Hot Spot for Me

*This is what the Lord says: "Let not the wise man boast of his wisdom or the strong man boast of his strength or the rich man boast of his riches, but let him who boasts boast about this: that he understands and knows Me, that I am the Lord, who exercises kindness, justice and righteousness on earth for in these I delight," declares the Lord.*
*Jeremiah 9:23-24*

Before leaving town, Bob and Jill had introduced me to one of their son's teachers, Beatrice, who promised to find a place for me to stay while I wait for the camper to be ready. I hadn't heard from Beatrice when I had expected to, so I called her. She said that a friend of hers has an extra apartment that he always rents out over the summer. This had me somewhat concerned. Not that I can't afford to rent an apartment, but money spent on rent and other luxuries can't be spent on ministry. Late yesterday afternoon Beatrice took me to the apartment, and it's a big (three bedroom!), beautiful apartment a block from the sea with a spectacular view from the fourth floor. Her friend, Massimo, never said a word about paying! So I settled in to enjoy Massimo's huge apartment overlooking the sea.

Then I walked back to Bob and Jill's house to tidy-up before her parents' arrival. When they arrived, close to midnight, I handed over the keys to the house and walked back to the apartment in the cool night air. It is a 40 minute walk, on the road that runs by the sea. There was a little salty breeze coming from the sea and the stars danced above.

Massimo's nice apartment has only one problem: there is no internet service. I'll have to go look for free Wi-Fi tomorrow because my internet hours are almost gone. Earlier today I went to McDonalds for free Wi-Fi close to where the camper is waiting to be inspected. On this Faith Trip it seems like I have spent more time in McDonalds than in all my years previously—spending far more time, but far less money there. I sure wish I could resist those French fries! God is good!

### Ireland

The Catholic Church once had massive influence over daily life in the past, but its influence is rapidly waning due to the sex abuse scandals, and a history of bloodshed that has often been portrayed as religious in origin. Ireland's population is very young compared to other European countries: 21% under age 15. Irish youth are plagued by alcoholism, suicide, broken families, alternative lifestyles, and post-Christian attitudes. Muslims are increasing faster than evangelicals. Travelers (Gypsies), numbering about 25,000, have been in Ireland for centuries, and tend to be poor, illiterate, and have the lowest life expectancy.

Pray for unity and continued growth within the Body of Christ, and that believers will be moved to reach out to the young, the poor, and the marginalized people of Ireland. (Operation World, pgs. 474-477.)

## Faith Trip - Day 26
## Journey to the End of Myself

*Remain in Me, and I will remain in you. No branch can bear fruit by itself; it must remain in the vine. Neither can you bear fruit unless you remain in Me.*
*John 15:4*

This morning I was on the terrace, having my first cup of coffee, and looking at the sparkling sea. I felt very grateful. Then I realized that I've been by the sea for over a week and I have taken exactly one walk on the beach. I haven't gotten so much as a toe wet.

I confess, I don't care so much for the sea. I grew up near San Francisco, where the current flows straight down from Alaska and the water is absolutely frigid. I remember that swimming in the Pacific Ocean required baby steps, with long pauses to let my feet, then ankles, then knees, legs, and stomach become numb with the cold. I don't remember ever getting past the stomach. And every time we hosted visitors from out of town, we would take them for a cruise around the San Francisco Bay. Every cruise ended in me vomiting. Each summer when I would go out for the first time, I got a sunburn that slowly evolved into a tan—not a good thing to do to yourself. Besides the health considerations, a sunburn is very uncomfortable. I have a high tolerance for pain, but a very low tolerance for irritations of the skin. And brings me to the other discomforts of the beach: salty water and sand. Even if my skin isn't already irritated with a sunburn, the salty water is irritating as it dries upon the skin. And sand has a tendency to get everywhere—I mean *everywhere*—which is tremendously irritating. And then the final point: I don't have a body that I want to show the world. Besides being overweight, I have always had a sense of body shame. And to go along with the body shame and skin irritation, there's shaving, which I haven't done in almost a year. For me the pleasures of a swim in the sea are just not worth the discomfort and irritation.

All of which brings me back to this morning: I sat there on the terrace, asking myself, "Why am I here?" After the Faith Trip I will be returning to spend a month by the sea in Bob and Jill's house. Why? There are so many people who would love to be here, who would enjoy swimming in the sea, who would swim daily; who would enjoy the sun, and would soak it up daily. Why am *I* here? Then I realized that perhaps God wants to do a work of healing for this irritability and body shame. Hmm . . . if that's the way it is, I will submit—and submerge. But enjoy it? Probably not.

Having a rest is a great thing, but obviously it has given me too much time to think. Is that necessarily a bad thing? I began to reflect on these negative emotions—and their fiendish source: frustration, irritation, shame, fear, self-doubt, self-loathing, depression, addiction, anger, denial, abandonment, self-pity—any emotion that is not rooted in selfless love. I realized that these things all have the same author: the father of lies, also known as the accuser, AKA the devil.

I felt like God was asking me who I wanted to believe, Him or the devil. Put that way, of course I choose to believe

God. And God spoke to my spirit: "You are precious, you're special, you're beautiful, and I love you. Now let go of all those lies you've believed about yourself all these years. There is nothing bad or ugly or shameful about you. You are My own lovely daughter. Your heart is pure: rich as cream and white as snow. Come and let Me heal your broken heart."

I remembered a sermon I heard a year earlier, in which God's love was described as a waterfall. Specifically, Niagara Falls, and His love, just like those waters, is massive and just keeps falling, falling, falling down on us. So I took a moment and thought of His love falling on me like Niagara Falls. It was wonderful. I could feel the sweet weight of that love. I allowed myself to really drink in His love, feeling love flowing back to Him from me.

Heaven, I thought, will be like this: an unbroken and unbreakable love bond with God. And in addition, it will be an everlasting adventure of discovery in which we will be allowed to explore all God's creation and search out all the wisdom and mystery of the universe—and universes and Heaven and heavens. All while enjoying the Niagara Falls of God's love and presence. John and Paul, when they were each taken up into Heaven (Revelation 4:1; I Corinthians 2:9), found that its beauty and wonder was indescribable.

Then I thought about my task to minister encouragement to missionaries throughout Europe. And I realized (not for the first time) my inadequacy. What qualification do I have for this work? I was a housewife and stay-at-home mother for

26 years, and before that I was a working mother. I never finished college. In every way I would be classified as an underachiever—a middle-aged underachiever. Suddenly I felt overwhelmed and a little scared because of the possibility, no, the *probability*, of failure if the task relied upon me.

But this is great news! Because my task is so impossibly huge, there's no way I can do it in my own strength. I must rely completely upon God. This task that is impossible for me is not impossible for God. I just need to be sure that I am always connected to Jesus, my Vine. Look, Listen, Love. Some days challenges are all inside of me, but God is good!

## Latvia

Latvia has a lot of European-style social problems stemming from the legacy of Communist atheism and nominal Christianity: alcohol, drugs, rapidly-growing sex trade, high abortion rate, the world's fourth highest suicide rate, and rampant corruption. The rural populations, Russian minority, and Jews (numbering about 7,000) are among the least-reached of the Latvian people.

Pray for effective and sensitive outreach, and for the trend toward unity to continue. (Operation World, pgs. 525-527.)

## Faith Trip - Day 27
## Into the Deep End

*I was afraid because I was naked; so I hid.*
*Genesis 3:10*

One of the biggest blessings in my life is my mom. She is super-supportive of my life and ministry in Europe, even though it has taken me far away from her. Many people tell me how brave I am to have moved to a foreign country alone. Mom's unfailing support is the reason why I can be so strong and brave. I was thinking of Mom because it is her 75th birthday today, though nobody would imagine that she's more than 60. Like me, Mom has a positive outlook on life and lots of energy. Just after Christmas, Mom was widowed for the second time in a decade.

As I was praying this morning, one of the local pastors, Paolo, came to mind with a sense of urgency. I contacted him to set up a time to meet with him and his wife, Monica. He said he would like to meet, but that he wasn't feeling well. I told him that I'll be praying for him to feel better. That may be why he came to my mind with an urgency. The Holy Spirit sometimes brings people to mind to pray for, but it's not always ours to know why. I'll go meet with Paolo and Monica tomorrow afternoon.

In anticipation of going for a swim in the sea, I bought sunscreen (# 30!) and razors, and shaved my legs. What I didn't buy (and have decided that I won't buy) is a swimsuit. I left mine in Texas. Instead I would go swimming in a T-shirt and trousers rolled up to the knee.

Not only would this save me the ordeal of swimsuit shopping (not fun even when I was young and thin), but it would also save my shoulders and back from getting sunburnt. And just to be extra sure, I waited for the afternoon sun to get low on the horizon before I went out. I also thought that it wouldn't be a bad thing if the beach cleared-out some, too.

As I approached the sea, the hardest part was choosing a place to leave my towel and glasses. God knows I need them, and nobody is going to mess with somebody's glasses, but sometimes it's the silliest things that stop us from doing what we know God has told us to do. I finally chose a spot and walked into the water. Along the way I saw (or I thought I saw!) what lookcd like a dead jellyfish on sand. I've been stung by a jellyfish. It's like a burn and an electrical shock together—electric fire, so I hesitated. Then I remembered that if God was telling me to take a swim in the sea, He would certainly protect me from jellyfish stings and everything else.

So on I went into the water. The water was clear, cool, and calm—not unpleasant at all! I was determined not to leave until I had gotten completely wet. When I reached waist-deep waters I began to swim. After swimming for a few minutes, I was ready to leave. But as I turned toward the beach I felt God in my spirit saying, "Lay back and relax." So I did, and I discovered something wonderful: I'm buoyant! I can float in a swimming pool without problems, but in the sea I float like beach ball. I love floating! So I was floating on my back for a good, long time, listening to the strange ticking sound of the sea and letting the waves rock me. It was fantastic!

When left the water, I picked up my towel and glasses and walked toward the stairs to the street. I passed a fisherman by his boat. He laughed and said, "Are you going to go back into the house like that?" Because I was fully dressed and soaking wet. I explained that I don't have a swimsuit. He pointed across the street and said, "For €10 you can buy one there."

I had to take a long walk before I finally stopped dripping enough to enter the apartment building. I went straight to the bathroom to shower the salt off my skin. I started thinking that maybe I should buy a swimsuit, after all. Hmm, it seems like I'm going to swim in the sea some more. But buy a swimsuit? God help me! I guess I'll have to do that, too, though I'd rather go to the dentist! But, I reminded myself, I've decided to let go of shame.

Honestly, I never thought that God would lead me to go for a swim in the sea. I am going to have to stop trying to predict what God is going to have me do—it's useless! His thoughts are definitely not my thoughts! God is good!

## Lithuania

Religious freedom in the post-Soviet era injected new life into the nation's spirituality, and unity among various Christian groups is very good. Freedom has also brought progress, but with it certain dangers: materialism, hedonism, and nihilism; and evils: substance abuse, suicide, and trafficking of women to the West for prostitution.

Pray for the good trends to continue, and for the evils to be exposed and wiped out. (Operation World, pgs. 541-543.)

## Faith Trip - Day 28
## A Perfect Fit

*Prayer does not fit us for the greater work; prayer is the greater work.*
*Oswald Chambers*

I went out this morning to use the free Wi-Fi at a nearby cafe. On the way (without letting myself think too much about it), I bought a swimsuit. I didn't let myself think too much about it because I knew that if I thought too much about it I would talk myself out of the idea altogether. The shopkeeper asked me what color—I hadn't thought about what color! I said, "Anything but black." She said, "That's refreshing! Everyone comes in wanting only black, black, black." But I know what my too-white flesh would look like in a black swimsuit—not good! She gave me three choices, and it was obvious that she had sized me up as soon as I entered the door. She asked me if I wanted to try them on and again without thinking[1] I said, "Yes." The one I picked was OK, though I'm sure it will never be my favorite thing to wear.

The laughing fisherman was wrong about the price, but I knew it would cost a whole lot more than €10 (maybe men's swimsuits cost (the equivalent of) €10—in 1960!). It came to €59, which is about what I thought it would cost.

---

[1] Just to clarify: I'm not advocating "not thinking" as a solution to problems. It's just that in this case, thinking too much was stopping me from doing what I believe God wanted me to do.

But that's a small thing (no pun intended!), the big thing was more interior work. I had told the Lord that I want to lose weight, and I am eating lighter foods. But weight is only a symptom of a much worse problem: idolatry. I had been using food for many years now as a source of comfort for feelings of loneliness, anxiety, anger, sorrow, shame, and fear. Last summer God took me for a lap around the wilderness because of the issue of food idolatry. At that time I told my friend, Suzy, about this issue, but she's thin and immediately took it to be a weight issue. She began to watch every bite of food that went into my mouth, and nearly drove me crazy. I repeat: weight is only a symptom. Food idolatry is not something you're likely to ever see anyone do because it's a thing done in isolation. Food idolaters aren't merely stuffing themselves with food, but they're stuffing down those negative emotions that are too hard to deal with. That was what God was dealing with today.

I had made myself a big salad for lunch, and as I was eating it, I felt the Holy Spirit telling me to slow down and really taste the food and feel the sensation of fullness in my stomach. I was going to have some tuna after the salad, but felt the urging of the Holy Spirit to stop and spend some time with God instead. So the tuna went into the fridge for later. I got Prayer Bear and gently knelt down on him (my left knee is still sore from my fall, and has turned lots of not-so-pretty colors). Despite the pain in my knee, I had a very enjoyable time with the Lord. I didn't blather on and on, as I sometimes do, but instead, just stayed quietly in His presence. It was wonderful! And the desire for more food vanished in the fullness of His love.

And I'll confess, I didn't want to write about the issue of food idolatry—especially after the way that Suzy had misunderstood it. But now that I have, I'm glad I did. It's not easy to be so honest about my faults. I wasn't always this honest, but I discovered that once you stop trying to "protect" yourself, and really open up to others, it becomes more comfortable (or less uncomfortable). I'm learning to let God be my Protector and my Defender.

Then I got ready for dinner with Paolo and his family. Sometime within the last few years he had been involved in an accident and almost died. Monica's parents are also a concern because of Alzheimer's. I prayed for them and for God to use me to comfort and encourage them. While praying for Paolo a few months ago, I saw a vision of Paolo preaching at many different pulpits. I believe that God was giving me a vision of his future, not his past: that he would again be preaching at many pulpits. I can't wait to tell him so. God is good!

## Macedonia

Macedonia is one of the poorest regions of the former Yugoslavia, plagued by high unemployment, and a low standard of living, the young and talented have mostly left. Segregation is more common than harmony among the ethnic groups:   the Orthodox Macedonians, Albanian Muslims, Romani (Gypsies), and the Turkish Muslims. Of these groups, the Romani are the poorest, least educated, and practice a superstitious version of Islam.

Pray for the optimistic church planting, evangelism, and missionary efforts, that they will bear fruit. (Operation World, pgs. 545-547.)

# Faith Trip - Day 29
## Prayer, Gratitude, & Progress

*Prayer is not overcoming God's reluctance, but laying
hold of His willingness.*
*Variously attributed*

Paolo and Monica served chicken barbequed Italian-style
with fragrant rosemary and crispy/creamy fried potatoes.
They talked about their struggles: Monica's aging parents,
Paolo's continuing, but slow recovery from the near-fatal
accident, and the subsequent halting of their ministry.
Paolo confided that if his life consists of merely preaching
without the power and presence of the Holy Spirit, he
doesn't think he can go on. This is something I understand
very well. In fact, it constituted one of the motivator for
this Faith Trip: living in the power and presence of the
Holy Spirit. I told him that I don't believe God called him
(or anyone) to preach apart from the power and presence of
the Holy Spirit. I also told him about my belief that the
vision of him preaching at many pulpits wasn't about the
past, but the future. He was greatly encouraged and we
prayed about all these issues. I also shared about Look,
Listen, Love.

As we said goodnight, they said that my visit had been very
encouraging, which in turn was encouraging for me. To
me, it doesn't seem like such a big thing: going to their
house, eating a delicious meal, and praying for their
concerns. In all this, I felt like I was the one who was
blessed. But that's our God! He loves to put people
together to bless each other. And since encouragement is

my ministry and my spiritual gifting, it's good to know that God is continuing to work through me.

This morning there was more interior work. My internet hours are used up for the month, so I had gone out to the Wi-Fi hotspots I know about here in the area. Today, none were working. So I ventured farther out, and still found none. Finally, in a big town in Le Marche (the next "state" or region), I asked the geekiest-looking guys around where I could find a Wi-Fi hotspot, and they didn't know of any. Finally, I gave the local cafe one last try at about 10:30 this evening, and the internet was finally functioning again.

With my need to connect satisfied, I came back to the apartment, reflecting on how, once again, I had become frustrated in the search. When I recognized those feelings of frustration today, I had surrendered and stopped the search. I started instead to thank God because even though I really wanted to check e-mail (more important than ever with a grandbaby due any day!), the reality of the situation was that I couldn't. When I finally surrendered I began to feel like I was back on track. After all, if it's truly important, won't God show me where to go to connect?

I had thought that the camper might be ready today, so I had tidied up and packed what I could, before heading out to look for Wi-Fi. But that call didn't come in. I still hoped to get the camper, deliver it to Bob in Switzerland, and get back to Romania in time to help with the outreach to Romanian gypsies with Jesus is the Answer (a different branch of the container folks in "Bunnyland" near Florence). But I'm pretty sure that the outreach is probably finishing up soon. All this had surely been a contributing factor in the frustration I was feeling today.

This frustration issue keeps coming back. I thought I was getting quicker about recognizing it, but most of the afternoon today was spent being frustrated instead of grateful. I am grateful, but I really needed to get over this frustration hurdle. It occurred to me that frustration is the opposite of gratitude. When I finally started thinking about all that I have to be grateful for, I began to feel very grateful indeed.

Just before the Faith Trip, I had the realization that each day I have at least 100 million things to be grateful for—many of which I never even think about, like having air to breathe and healthy lungs to breathe with, that this air is invisible so that I can see my way around, that sometimes a cool breeze refreshes me or brings in a little rain to clean the street, etc. Every day of my life I had been taking the air for granted, but there are many, many other things to be grateful about every day. Gratitude, I realized, is not only the opposite, it's the antidote to frustration. I need to work at it because gratitude is not reflexive for me (not yet, anyway!).

Then I thought: "Maybe the camper will be ready tomorrow." But if not, I have resolved to be grateful for another weekend by the beautiful Adriatic Sea. God is working in everything for the good, and that's because God is good!

## Malta

Malta was the first nation in Europe to embrace Christianity when the Apostle Paul was shipwrecked on the island, and it is the most religious nation in Europe, with a majority who regularly attend mass and over 80% who feel that their religion is important to them. However, few Maltese have a personal walk with the living Lord Jesus.

Pray that the Holy Spirit will breathe new life into religious tradition, and for maximum impact from the Alpha Course and the JESUS film. (Operation World, pgs. 568-570.)

## Faith Trip - Day 30
## Floating on His Promise

*"Be still and know that I am God."*
*Psalm 46:10a*

My first grandchild is due is three weeks. Naturally, the coming birth has been on my mind a lot lately. The parents don't know whether it's a boy or a girl, and don't want to know. I like that they feel that way. I didn't want to know with my pregnancies, either. The surprise was as much fun as the arrival (well once the labor is all done, that is!). While praying for my grandchild shortly after hearing news of the pregnancy, all feminine pronouns came out of my mouth without having given the issue any thought. I told Josh, my son, he said, "We've chosen dozens of girl names and not one single boy name." We'll see! Whatever, this baby will be loved and welcomed.

I have not planned to return to the US right away after the baby is born. Instead, I've booked flights for a visit in September—just about the time maternity leave will be ending. I wish the US had generous maternity (and paternity) leave like Italy. But I'll be there to help out and to give the new parents a bit of a break.

I still haven't heard about the camper. Praise God for another weekend at the beach! I was struggling a little with those negative emotions again today, but spent time with God instead of letting them drag me down. Too much time to think is like fertile ground: the weeds can spring up and start to take root. Carrying that metaphor a little further, I guess I need to get into my mind's garden, pull up the weeds, and plant something good in their place. I decided to read until it was time to go for my evening swim. Have you ever noticed how God puts the right book in your hand at just the right time?

A warm wind has blown in from the south, bringing with it humid, gray clouds and the possibility of rain. As I was floating I remembered how, back in Budapest (Day Three), Klaus had prophesied to me, saying, "Give me your hands," and then telling me to relax, as he began to rock my hands back and forth. At that moment, floating on my back, it occurred to me that his rocking motion was just like the motion of the waves. He had said that God was telling me to relax and rest in Him. I don't know why I hadn't remembered it before, but I realized that it had been a prophetic word for swimming in the sea as much as for the rest of the Faith Trip. I also realized that as much as letting go of the tension in my body, I needed to let go of that feeling that I need to be "in control" (probably a contributing factor in feelings of frustration).

It's not easy. How can something so simple like relaxing and resting and trusting be so difficult? I have no illusions about being more competent than God. And control is not something I normally struggle about with others. In fact, if I'm not driving, I almost always fall asleep—so non-existent is my need for control. As I lay floating on the tranquil sea's breast I made a mental note to work on resting. Immediately, I burst out laughing at the silly idea of "working at" learning to rest!

When I returned to the apartment I called Massimo and asked if I could extend my stay until Monday morning. He said yes. I thought: "Who knows? Maybe I'll be spending Monday night in the camper!" If not, then I'll go back to Bob and Jill's house. And I realized that I'm fine either way it goes. I am willing to let go of the idea of meeting up with the team in Romania. God will bring many other opportunities to serve. I thought: "I guess I'm learning to be more flexible about my plans." And then I realized that this time alone with Him is my chance to be equipped for greater work. With that thought, Romania became easy to finally let go. Someday, someday! God is really, really good!

## Moldova

Moldova is Europe's poorest nation due to political problems, lack of industry and trade, economic dependence on Russia and the lingering effects of Communism. Unemployment and alcohol abuse are big problems, and the depressed economy has forced up to 25% of Moldovans to seek work abroad. Moldova is the source of the largest numbers of young women lured into human trafficking rings. Despite (or perhaps because of all) this, Moldova is very fertile ground for the gospel, with churches growing and multiplying.

Pray for effective outreach to all, including those less-reached (the Gagauz, the Muslim minorities, and the

Gypsies) and for the love of God to reach all Moldovans. (Operation World, pgs. 590-592.)

## Faith Trip - Day 31
## Summer Came in on the Wind

*It is well said that "asking is the rule of the kingdom." It is a rule that will never be altered in anybody's case. If the royal and divine Son of God cannot be exempted from the rule of asking that He may have, you and I cannot expect the rule to be relaxed in our favor.*
*C.H. Spurgeon*

Today was the day that summer came to Monte Pannolini. The warm southern breeze that blew in yesterday hadn't brought rain, but it did make the temperature jump about 5° (to 95° Fahrenheit). I cranked out the awning on the terrace, closed the shutters on the sunny side of the house, and spent the day trying to keep cool. I was spending some time with Prayer Bear and God after lunch when I suddenly remembered that I had seen a fan in the attic. I hadn't been snooping—there is no door on the attic, so it was easy to see that there was a fan up there. I also remembered that there was a ladder by the washer. I climbed up to the attic and brought down the fan. The fan will definitely help me sleep better tonight.

Today is prayer for India day by Operation World. While praying for India (specifically for the many, many unreached people groups) I was moved to tears for this sub-continent. At the Hope for Europe conference, someone had said that if you have a vision for your mission field, then you must look beyond it. I think the reason, perhaps, is that God doesn't want us to become myopic in the vision for our mission field. We need to see our mission

117

field and how it fits in with the rest of God's world[2].

"Everyone who has left houses or brothers or sisters or father or mother or children or fields for My sake will receive a hundred times as much and will inherit eternal life," (Matthew 19:29). While praying for my unborn grandchild, this verse came to my mind. When I had that important talk with Kevin in Florence (about how I am not running away from my problems), I was aware of the cost of being so far away from family—especially now that Josh, my other son, is about to make me a grandmother. I am torn, really torn. And I feel that tearing as a physical pain, right in the middle of my heart.

But I know, too, that I couldn't stay in the US no matter how much I would like to. I am very aware that time is running out for this world. When I go to the US, I enjoy visiting family and friends, but in the back of my mind I hear the clock ticking down the time for Jesus' return. I've sacrificed a lot to be here, but I couldn't have done anything else.

A prophet told me that I was called from the womb like Jeremiah. I know it's true. I've known it all my life (without knowing what it was or what it meant). Having a calling is a great and terrible thing. It's great because there

---

[2] If you want to pray for the world, Operation World is a valuable resource for how to pray specifically country-by-country for the world. You can find Operation World in book form through Amazon or connect online at www.operationworld.org.

is a clarity of purpose that makes it easier to brush away doubts and fears. And it's a terrible thing because it's a tremendous burden. There's a sense of responsibility and urgency that makes it impossible to go on living a "normal" life. It's also a terrible thing because people who don't have your vision and your calling don't understand you (again, look at Jeremiah). But if you think about it, how could they possibly understand?

I'm not special. Not at all. As you no doubt know by now, I am a flawed human being—and nobody knows that better than I do. You have a calling, too, though you may not know it. Seek God if you don't know your calling. A good place to start (where I started) is by learning what your spiritual gifts. Take a spiritual gifts test. I recommend the one written by C. Peter Wagner. It will open your eyes. When you learn what your spiritual gift is, then look for opportunities to use that gift. God will give you opportunities that will surprise and bless you. You'll never know greater joy than working with God and being right in the center of His will for your life.

My prayer for the day: Let my life be a proof of what the omnipotent God can do through an ordinary, flawed woman. Amen!

## Monaco & San Marino

Both countries enjoy great wealth thanks to tourism. Monaco is also a tax haven and gambling destination, while San Marino deals more in banking. Monaco has a small group of evangelical believers now for the first time, but in San Marino evangelism hardly exists because past outreaches resulted in jailing or expulsion from the country. Both countries are nominally Catholic.

Pray for a life-changing encounter with the living Lord Jesus Christ in both countries that will counter the deception of materialism and the dependence on wealth. (Operation World, pgs. 593-594; 725-726.)

## Faith Trip - Day 32
## Learning the Fine Art of Waiting

*It is good to wait quietly for the salvation of the Lord.*
*Lamentations 3:26*

Today was moving day. I had been at Massimo's apartment for a week, while Jill's parents were in town. Her parents went back home tonight, and the timing couldn't have been better because Massimo needed to have the apartment back.

Between moves I had six hours to kill, which I did at the Wi-Fi cafe. The folks at the internet cafe are very nice and don't mind me spending all day there. Killing time without an internet connection is tougher, but doable.

Jill's parents are lovely, sweet people. They had invited me out for brunch one day—fragrant, flaky brioches and foamy cappuccinos. As I was praying for them this morning, it occurred to me that I could have invited them out for a pizza or something, but the opportunity is gone now. And I realized almost immediately that the reason I hadn't invited them out is because I still haven't learned how to live gracefully as a single in a world of couples. I am fine eating in a restaurant alone. But when I go out with a couple, I still feel like a fifth wheel—useless and absurd. The really strange part of it is that I frequently went out alone with couples when I was married, and it never bothered me. It's something I will just have to learn to handle.

I wonder how many other times I've failed to invite people out when I should have. Or how many times people who seem closed are actually like me, just feeling unsure of their place. God give me grace and help me to be more gracious and generous with others.

I still haven't heard a word about the camper. I've let go of Romania, but I'm feeling antsy and anxious to get back to work. And having too much time on my hands has given me too much time to think. Those negative thoughts haven't stopped creeping in. As Joyce Meyer observed, the mind is a battleground. Mine certainly is. While praying, I had realized how much—and how often—I need God. I tend to go along, thinking everything is OK, but without His guidance and His help, I am lost. Jesus really does hold everything together: all the big things, all the small things, all the things we never think about—everything, including my sanity! I don't want to live on autopilot, just coasting along. I want to live deliberately in and with and for Him and His kingdom. But it's so easy to lose the way. How precious and valuable is what the Holy Spirit had taught me about Look, Listen, Love.

"Oh, please, Lord," I prayed, desperation oozing out of my pores in big, greasy drops. "Help me to live in You: Look, Listen, Love! And if You would, please speed up the work on the camper!" His response? Relax and float while you're waiting. Nothing could be simpler—or harder to do! But as always, God is good!

# Montenegro

Despite the enmity between ethnic/religious communities that has characterized most of the Balkans, Montenegro shows great potential, particularly as a tourist destination. The Montenegrin Orthodox Church has sought to establish itself in place of the Serbian Orthodox Church. The evangelical community is small, but growing.

Pray for effective outreach and sensitivity, particularly with regard to the ethnic minorities: Bosniak Muslims, Albanians, and the Romani (Gypsies). Also pray for more foreign missionaries to be sent to Montenegro, which is mostly overlooked. (Operation World, pgs. 597-599.)

## Faith Trip - Day 33
## Rejoicing! If They Could, So Can I!

*Rejoice in the Lord always. I will say it again: Rejoice! Let your gentleness be evident to all. The Lord is near. Do not be anxious about anything, but in everything, by prayer and petition, with thanksgiving, present your requests to God. And the peace of God, which transcends all understanding, will guard your hearts and your minds in Christ Jesus.*
*Philippians 4:4-7*

While reading the Bible this morning I suddenly became aware of what a complainer I am. Here I am living a block from the beautiful Adriatic Sea and all I can do is complain about waiting for the camper and about my battle against negative thoughts. And here's what gave me my reality check: "The apostles left the Sanhedrin, rejoicing because they had been counted worthy of suffering disgrace for the Name," (Acts 5:41). These men had been stripped and publicly flogged—and they rejoiced! What a whiny baby I am! Obviously, I need to get better at this waiting thing!

And almost as soon as I got that reality check, the camper guy called and said that the camper is ready. We set tomorrow morning as a time to meet. I'll soon be back on the road and back in action!

The sea was very agitated today, but there's a breakwater that keeps the shore area calm. So instead of big breakers, there were little choppy waves, carrying the salty perfume of the sea. As I floated, God (who rarely repeats Himself) kept saying, Relax! Relax! You know how someone will tell you to relax, and they gently shake you by the arm? Well, the little waves moved each of my limbs separately from the others, like God was shaking every part of me, trying to get me to relax. And it worked! But it was also so funny that I started laughing. I felt like I was going through Lamaze classes all over again, only this time I'm not pregnant, and God is my coach. So there I was floating and laughing, relaxed as I have ever been, and feeling loved. Who couldn't love a God so sweet and funny? And again, I thought of Klaus, holding my hands and gazing deep into my eyes. In those liquid brown eyes I saw the patient, passionate gaze of my loving Lord Jesus.

Then I checked my e-mail while fixing dinner (borrowing a bit of the neighbor's unsecured network). A Bulgarian missionary who I only know through the internet saw I was online and sent me a link over Skype. I opened the link and it was live streaming of a worship service in English. As the praise music washed over me my heart opened in adoration of my Lord. And I realized that this is what has been missing from my life lately: just the pure love for my Lord. I had been all focused on doing, going, and growing in my walk. Not that those are bad things, but like Martha I had somehow missed the bigger purpose of my life: loving and being loved by my Creator. It all keeps coming back to the simple things. I need to sit at His feet, listen to His voice, and enjoy His presence. Those other things will follow as I keep focused on the more important things. God is good!

## Netherlands

In the Netherlands there is freedom of religion, but also freedom for almost any lifestyle. The country has turned from its Christian heritage to become a decadent, secular society, openly permissive of homosexuality and abortion. The Netherlands was the first country to legalize euthanasia. What appears as tolerance turns out to be mostly indifference, with once-liberal immigration policies tightening in the wake of murder and a failure to integrate into Dutch life and society.

Pray for spiritual renewal and dynamism, a recommitment to Scripture and Biblical holiness in contrast to liberalism and tolerant pluralism. (Operation World, pgs. 624-627.)

## Faith Trip - Day 34
## Yay! Camper!

*You do not test the resources of God until you attempt the impossible.*
*F.B. Meyer*

I took the train to the meeting point that camper guy had named: McDonalds in a nearby town. I was early but so was camper guy. (Camper guy does have a name, but Bob and I have gotten into the habit of calling him camper guy, and it's just easier to remember him this way.) He drove me up the narrow, winding dirt road to the camper inspection station. The camper inspector was probably in his mid-thirties. He had a massive beer gut and hairless, sunburnt arms and chest. He pointed to a spot by the back gate, and there she was: my camper! She was the smallest and prettiest camper there.

You read that right, the camper is feminine. We've named her the Duchess because she has her boyfriend's name (Granduca) tattooed on her forehead (she's punk!). Actually, Granduca means Grand Duke, and it's a model name for Fiat.

Camper guy showed me around, with practical things like how to turn on and off the stove, water pump, heater, etc. I climbed into the driver's seat and saw that she has a column shift. Camper guy showed me how a column shift works. It's easy—exactly like a floor shift set sideways. I hadn't actually bought the camper yet. To this point I only had the down-payment on it. Finally, we got down to the paperwork, and an hour later, she was mine.

I drove back to Bob and Jill's house, loaded up the Duchess, and set out on the road. I wanted to get to Milan tonight, if possible. The first thing to do was to gas up. There was a helpful young attendant who pumped for me even though I had pulled into the self-service pumps.

As I pulled back onto the highway, something seemed not quite right. About a mile down the road, things were worse, she was losing power and belching great clouds of smoke. I pulled into the next gas station, barely making it to an out of the way spot before she coughed and the engine died.

I called camper guy and described the problem. He said that it sounds like the kid had pumped diesel fuel instead of gasoline. I had forgotten to tell him *benzina* (gasoline). Camper guy suggested calling the insurance, but they said that it's not covered.

I'm writing this as I wait for a mechanic to tow the camper to his garage. Because I was on the highway, I must have gotten about ten miles down the road before I had the opportunity to turn off. So they're going to have to flush the whole system, change the gas filter, and clean out the carburetor. All of which may take a few more days.

In spite of all this, I'm feeling surprisingly calm. Maybe it's because God told me: Relax! Relax! the other day. I do feel relaxed. I didn't get very far from Bob and Jill's house, so I guess I'll find a way to get back there. This is certainly not how I had thought this day would go! But I do feel very calm and relaxed.

I have resolved to find a marker and write *SOLO BENZINA* (only gasoline) in bold letters above the gas cap. I can assure you, I will never make this mistake again!

~          **Four Hours Later**          ~

The camper is fixed! Oh praise God! I was pretty sure this would mean I would have to spend another weekend here. I was also pretty sure it was going to be fairly expensive. But I just stayed calm and grateful.

The girls at the gas station cafe (mother and daughter) were super-nice to me. After my call to the insurance got turned down, they called their mechanic for me. It was like seeing God's mercy and love gazing at me through the clear, blue eyes of the teenaged girl and her mother. After I had waited over two hours for the mechanic, they brought me a cool glass of water. Then an hour later they brought me a plate full of delicious appetizers and another cool glass of water. "Anyone who welcomes you welcomes Me, and anyone who welcomes Me welcomes the one who sent Me. Whoever welcomes a prophet as a prophet will receive a prophet's reward, and whoever welcomes a righteous person as a righteous person will receive a righteous person's reward. And if anyone gives even a cup of cold water to one of these little ones who is My disciple, truly I tell you, that person will certainly not lose their reward," (Matthew 10:40-42).

Then the mechanic arrived without a tow truck and started

129

poking around the gas tank and looked under the hood. Another mechanic came and about an hour later, I saw the two of them push the duchess to the nearest gas pump. They asked me if they could fill the tank and I said yes. They filled it and drove it back to a parking place. She made a lot of smoke, but she ran! And the repair bill? €60! I had thought it could be hundreds!

The mechanics said I should go back to that gas station and complain. I asked for a receipt for the repair, but they said only their boss can write receipts. So they took me and the duchess to their garage. The boss was super-nice, too. He wrote up a receipt, spelling out exactly what happened. As he was writing out the receipt, I borrowed a marker from his desk and wrote over the gas tank *BENZINA* in big, block letters.

I decided to return to the gas station to ask them to refund me for the diesel fuel as well as for the repair. But between us, I'll settle for the diesel fuel cost. I sure am glad that I got receipts for all this!

By the time all this was finished, I decided to go back to Bob and Jill's house for the night, rather than start off at 7:30 in the evening. Tomorrow, after a visit to that gas station, I'll be on the road for real!

Today's lesson is that even when things seem to go horribly wrong, blessings and mercy are there in the midst of it all! God is good!

# Norway

The Lutheran Church (called the Church of Norway) is the official state church, and the most evangelical of all state churches in Europe. However, the church faces the same pluralistic challenges as other European society, and internal battle over homosexuality. Church planting is a real need in a society where church membership is high, but actual belief and attendance are low.

Pray for outreach, particularly to the minorities: the Sami, the largely Muslim immigrant minority, Asians, and immigrants from former Communist countries. Pray that church-planting and efforts will focus on Oslo, the key to Norway. (Operation World, pgs. 653-655.)

# Faith Trip - Day 35
## Starting Again

*We demolish arguments and every pretension that sets*
*itself up against the knowledge of God, and we take captive*
*every thought to make it obedient to Christ.*
*II Corinthians 10:5*

The Duchess passed the night on the beach road behind the
house blocking the driveway to Bob and Jill's house. Of
course, I knew nobody would complain. Besides, there was
no other place to park.

I slept very well, and woke early this morning. I set out
once again, and went back to the gas station where the kid
had pumped the diesel fuel. I asked to speak to the
manager, but he wasn't expected in for another couple of
hours. I said that I would wait, but the woman working the
pumps insisted on calling him. He lived in another town,
about 40 minutes away, so it would take him some time to
arrive. I got a coffee and waited in the gas station cafe.

As I waited, several negative thoughts tried to enter my
mind:

- That he would laugh and tell me it was my own
  fault for not watching what the boy was putting in
  the gas tank.

- Several highway police officers came in for
  coffee, and with them the thought that he might
  call the police on me.

- That he would throw me off his property—maybe even pull a gun on me.

And several other thoughts just as silly and paranoid. But as each of these thoughts came, I shoved them out of my mind, saying to myself: "But I have God Almighty on my side." And I reminded myself of God's instructions to Relax! Relax! And I found that I was relaxed, grateful, and trusting in God when the manager arrived 45 minutes later.

He asked to see the repair receipt. I showed him that and the receipt for the diesel fuel. He shrugged and said, "Oh, well! This is why we have insurance." He made a photocopy of the receipts. Then he went and opened the till and paid me the full €133 in cash and shook my hand. He even thanked me and invited me to come look him up next time I'm in the area.

I had a full gas tank, but I wanted to fuel up the duchess's other gas tanks because she also runs off LPG. In the southern part of Italy I had been told that LPG is difficult to find. It turns out that it's easy to find on the national highways, which is what I would be driving on all day. I watched the young man fuel up the LPG tanks (there are two of them), and it looked difficult. I commented on this, and he told me that because it's dangerous to handle, they have to be trained how to fuel up LPG tanks. I was relieved to hear that there's no self-service for LPG because it really does look complicated. And not only that, but every time they unhook the LPG spigot from the gas tank it sprays them with a fine mist of gas. No thanks! I wonder what health consequences this has for people who are sprayed with gas all day long, day after day, year after year. It can't be good.

Finally, a day after I bought her, the duchess and I were on the road. The highway from Monte Pannolini to Rimini had us climbing lots of hills and going through tunnels. The Duchess is like me: she's an old girl that slows down on the hills, but she chugs determinedly on and eventually makes it to the top. Naturally, I kept to the slow lane with the trucks and other campers. I stopped frequently on the way for water. Because of the heat, my high adrenaline, and hot flashes, I needed to stay well-hydrated.

When I got to her town, I wanted to stop by and visit Carla, but the GPS wasn't working. Since I had been to her house twice now, I thought I knew the way, but soon it was obvious that I had gotten badly off track. So I called her and we visited on the phone for a little bit before I returned to the highway and headed on to Milan. In Milan I need to get some things out of storage for the camper. My things were being stored in Guido's underground garage. When I had called, asking to get into the garage, Guido had invited me to have dinner with him.

Parking in Milan can be a problem, but I had prayed, so I knew that God would provide a place for the camper. I circled the block twice and called Guido. He said, "You've circled twice, right?" He had been looking at the street from his balcony and seen me. On the third pass, a place opened up that was perfect for the camper, and close to Guido's house.

As soon as I entered and sat down, Guido offered to let me stay the night in his spare bedroom. I gladly accepted, though I had been prepared to sleep in the camper. He fixed me a delicious meal of tortellini and beef cutlet.

Guido's daughter, Ilaria, and her family are the ones who have been hosting Boo-Boo, my kitty, since May. They live in the apartment just under his. After dinner I had a joyous reunion with Boo-Boo. She is obviously very happy staying with them. They were a big answer to prayer because being without an apartment is more of a problem for her than it is for me. Our original agreement was for Boo-Boo to stay with them possibly the whole summer. I told Ilaria: "I will be in the US for five months this winter, getting my house there ready to sell. Can you keep her for the winter, too?" Ilaria sadly shook her head and said no. She said that the problem is the litter box. They need to keep her litter box on the balcony because Ilaria has a very weak stomach. I said that I understand and returned to Guido's apartment to pray about the problem. I know I can't put Boo-Boo through the trauma of another 11 hour flight to the US, and then back again. I'll just have to find something else to do with her. I decided not to worry about it, but to put her into God's hands.

A few minutes later, Ilaria called me and said: "I know what to do! We'll cut a hole in the glass of the balcony door and install a kitty door for her." I said, "You would be willing to do that for her?" She said, "Of course!"

Now that I think of it, I have a bunch of things I need to do while I'm here in Milan. Bob doesn't need the camper for a few days, so it really doesn't make sense to rush about and leave this evening to go to Switzerland. Guido says that I can stay another night. That means that I can also visit my Italian home church tomorrow morning. For this I am very grateful! God is good! God is very, very good!

Pray for the health of the men and women in Italy and around the world who pump LPG for a living.

## Poland

The Catholic Church has long played a central role in Poland's national identity, and Poland is one of the most religious states in Europe. But since the death of Polish Pope John Paul II, regular mass attendance has dropped by about half. In addition, Polish Catholics are particularly devoted to Mary, and consider her the spiritual queen of Poland. The multiplication of foreign sects and religions has brought confusion. Jehovah's Witnesses outnumber evangelicals two to one. New Age, Pagan, and Wicca beliefs are growing and mixing with Catholic beliefs.

Pray for evangelicals to rise to the challenge in Poland, and for an end to secular materialism, particularly among the youth. (Operation World, pgs. 689-691.)

## Faith Trip - Day 36
## Home Sweet Home!

*Like a bird that flees its nest is anyone who flees from home.*
*Proverbs 27:8*

Being back in Milan has made me realize that I love this city like no other. Perhaps that's because it has been home (off and on) since 2001—the longest time in my life to ever call any place home. I was born in an age when the majority of Americans lived their whole lives within 50 miles of the place where they were born. As I grew up, that began to change, and more Americans have become like me. I have never lived in the same town for more than seven years my whole life, and most of my moves have been long-distance moves (more than 500 miles). Milan is the only place that I have ever moved back to after moving away. And although I currently don't have a home here (unless you count the Duchess!), I believe that I will someday again call Milan home.

I enjoyed this morning's church service immensely. It was marvelous to be welcomed back by my friends—my family! I must have been kissed 50 times before the service started. Many of these dear people have been praying for me and for this Faith Trip, following my adventures via e-mail, Facebook, and the blog. Still, they were anxious to hear about it all first hand. Many asked where the camper is parked, looking for it in the church parking area. But I had come across town on the subway, which is usually faster than driving.

The sermon was so close to home for me that it might as well have been titled: <u>A Message for Alisa</u>. The Bible reading was Luke 10:38-42:

> As Jesus and his disciples were on their way, he came to a village where a woman named Martha opened her home to him. She had a sister called Mary, who sat at the Lord's feet listening to what he said. But Martha was distracted by all the preparations that had to be made. She came to him and asked, "Lord, don't you care that my sister has left me to do the work by myself? Tell her to help me!"

> "Martha, Martha," the Lord answered, "you are worried and upset about many things, but few things are needed—or indeed only one. Mary has chosen what is better, and it will not be taken away from her."

The pastor said that Milan (the financial capital of Italy) might as well be called Marthaland because of all the busy-ness of business, work, fashion, shopping, finance, keeping up appearances, and running here and there. And even a lot of Christians are Marthas, busy doing this and that for God: prayer groups, Bible studies, soup kitchens, and attending every church event there is. These are all good things, as is work, but often God has not directed us to *do* all these things. And the part that really hit home with me was when she said that sometimes we take Marthaland on vacation with us, running up and down the beach doing, doing, doing. (Sounds like my last two weeks on the

138

beach!) The thing, the only thing we really need to do is to spend time at His feet, listening to His voice. And as I reflected on this, I came back to Look, Listen, Love, and Relax! Relax! Would it be wrong to say that I'm *working* on it?

And Milan is more like the rest of Europe than it is like the rest of Italy. For those of you who aren't aware, Europe can truly be called post-Christian. Many people here are so disillusioned by traditional Christianity that they have ceased to believe in God. Some have even actively embraced atheism and other beliefs that are contrary to Christianity. Many people (myself included) believe that traditional Christianity must change, and Christians must become missional in our thinking. Attractional church simply doesn't work for everybody. There are people out there who would love to have a relationship with God, but they hate church. Why does church have to be a prerequisite for getting into Heaven? Is that even in the Bible? We were always meant to be missional. Jesus called us to be salt and light in the world.

While walking on Corso Buenos Aires yesterday, I found myself in the middle of the crowd that had gathered to watch Milan's Gay Pride parade. I watched the crowd and the parade participants and for a moment felt the enormous, heartbreaking love of God for these people. Unlike many Christians who keep their distance, I believe that Jesus would have been (and actually was!) right there with me in that crowd. He was criticized by the religious people of His time for hanging out with prostitutes and tax collectors. But Jesus loved people. He loved spending time with those He would eventually die to redeem. I believe that if we can't love gays, we need to seriously examine our souls before God.

The heat of the day drove me back to Guido's house where I rested for about an hour. I'm not sure if it was a dream or a vision, but as I drowsed, I prayed for the crowd on Corso Buenos Aires. I prayed for each person that entered my mind's eye, and I saw each of them surrounded in an instant by a giant bubble which carried them heavenward. Most seemed unaware of their bubble, continuing to walk as if they were still on the ground. But the ones that did notice the bubble were amazed by it. They touched it delicately, and the bubble held. I saw one that tried to escape the bubble, but that bubble also held. I'm not sure what it means, but I'm sure the bubbles must represent either prayers or perhaps God's love because I was praying for each person as each one's bubble appeared. And again I felt His mighty, mighty love for each person.

A friend told to me that her church has started having commitment ceremonies for gay couples. This, in my opinion, is wrong. It puts the church's stamp of approval on a sinful lifestyle. God's Word calls homosexuality an abomination—a very strong word indeed! Remember, God is not a man that He should lie nor a son of man that He should change His mind (Numbers 23:19). He is the same yesterday, today, and forever (Hebrews 13:8). His stance on homosexuality, therefore, has not and will not change.

Nevertheless, I am not against civil commitment ceremonies for gay couples because I believe that if they

140

are committed to the lifestyle, it's not a bad thing to be committed to each other. It's far better than living the promiscuous lifestyle that resulted in the tragic spread of the AIDS virus.

Back to Jesus, our perfect example: although we don't have any recorded encounters with gays, look at the woman caught in the act of adultery. She was brought before Jesus to be condemned. Jesus refused to condemn her. Instead He invited those without sin to throw the first stone. Then He knelt down and began writing in the dirt. What did He write? It's not recorded, but possibly His writing was seen differently by each person there. The thief probably saw the word Theft, the liar may have seen the word Lies, etc. One after another, they dropped their stones and walked away. Then He stood up again and asked the woman where her accusers were. She told Him that they were gone, and He said to her, "Neither do I accuse you, *go and sin no more*," (John 8:11, emphasis mine).

We are called to a life of purity—a lifestyle which is impossible for *any of us* without the power of the Holy Spirit. I repeat: if we cannot love gay people, then we need to seriously examine our souls before God Almighty in sincere humility. It's a fine line. We need to love them, but how tragic would it be to love them only in our human way? And how tragic to go the other way and condemn them like the Pharisees with the adulterous woman. It has been said many times before: hate the sin, but love the sinner. I would turn that around and say love the person, but hate the sin. And no sin is worse than another. All sin is equally wrong in God's eyes. Some Christians despise

141

gays, yet listen to preachers who are unrepentant idolaters of money.

I don't know where I'll be sleeping tonight, but I have already given that need to God Almighty. He'll take care of me tonight and always. God is good!

## Portugal

Portugal has enjoyed freedom of religion since 1974, but with freedom come perils from materialism, individualism, and substance abuse, as well as infiltration by Jehovah's Witnesses, Mormons, and New Age beliefs. The evangelical community is hampered by serious divisions, and the need for a united vision, a passion for the lost, and church planting efforts. Ethnic minorities are largely unreached, and the gospel has little or no penetration into the seven northern and northeastern provinces, the four southern provinces the 316 counties (44 of which have no evangelical presence at all), and Madeira Island. Young people are also often spiritually neglected, with drug abuse as a sad result.

Pray for unity, outreach and church planting efforts, and for a vision for the youth. (Operation World, pgs. 692-694.)

## Faith Trip - Day 37
## Missional?

*People will be lovers of themselves, lovers of money,*
*boastful, proud, abusive, disobedient to their parents,*
*ungrateful, unholy, without love, unforgiving, slanderous,*
*without self-control, brutal, not lovers of the good,*
*treacherous, rash, conceited, lovers of pleasure rather*
*than lovers of God.*
*II Timothy 3:2-4*

Almost immediately after writing yesterday's installment,
Pina invited to stay with them. I knew that their door was
always open to me, but that does depend on somebody
being there to open it for me! How nice to be able to enjoy
the rest of the day without stressing over something like
that! I'm learning to put it into God's hands and rest fully
in helpless dependence and confident assurance that God
Almighty will take care of my needs. Since I've stopped
trying to solve my own problems, God has never, ever let
me down. In fact, He has taken even greater care of me
because of my complete dependence. It's something so
contrary to logic that it takes a good deal of discipline to do
something that should be really easy.

What I wrote yesterday about the importance of becoming
missional in our thinking was something I actually saw on
the subway on the way back to Guido's apartment after
church. I noticed a couple studiously reading books fat
enough to be Bibles. I stepped closer and saw that the
writing in both their books was in 2 column format, further
confirming that these were Bibles. I stepped in front of the

man and was able to read the title at the top of the page: *Genesi* (Genesis). So I commented that seeing people reading the Bible on the subway was a rather unusual sight. The man pulled out his ear buds and I repeated what I had said. They were sweet people, clearly committed to Christ. They told me about their church: an evangelical mission church from South America, with services in Spanish and Italian.

Later as I was thinking about and praying for this couple and their church, I realized that I had done exactly the same thing about six months ago. I rode the subway, my ears filled with Christian music, reading either the Bible or a Christian book. And God had told me to stop going around Milan like this: disconnected from the world in which I'm called to be salt and light. He showed me that although it's good to be plugged into Him, I shouldn't be disconnected from the world. This is the Look part of Look, Listen, Love. The Love part should be my response to what I see: prayers lifted up with passion and in compassion for those around me. I would have missed these two if I had been plugged-in and tuned-out.

I saw an ugly scene this morning as I headed out to do some errands. I was waiting for the bus. It was only 9:30 or so, but already scorching hot. An older woman (probably in her 70's) came up to me and we shared the scant shade of the bus stop sign with a young man. She started complaining about there not being a proper bus stop with a shade and seat. But the bus arrived almost immediately. I got on while she continued complaining to the young man. There was a stroller filling the aisle by the ticket stamping machine. I stamped my ticket and went to the middle of the bus to sit. The complainer got on and the bus started quickly (as they frequently do). She lost her balance and stumbled over the stroller. She was not injured, and she only stumbled, she did not fall. But she began screaming at the mother and grandmother of the child in the stroller about blocking the aisle. It's a scene I have seen from time to time, but this time it spun completely out of control. The complainer, I had observed, was already in a nasty mood. She was screaming so loudly that the bus driver told her to be quiet. She moved back to where I was sitting and found a seat across the aisle from me. She continued to complain loudly and began turning her rage against foreigners (the stroller people were probably from South America). She tried to engage me in her rage, and I refused to be drawn into it. Eventually she found a woman who agreed with her. And with this her waning rage found new strength and she became loud again. The grandmother came running back to where we were, got right in her face, and started screaming at the complainer. The two of them were joined by a middle-aged man. Meanwhile I started speaking: "*Pace, Pace*" (Peace, Peace) over the scene. And I believe that it is only because I, as a daughter of the King of Kings, was proclaiming peace over the situation that it never got physically violent. Because such was their rage that they were almost to the point of exchanging punches. The Bible says that in the end times there will be rage, and I certainly saw that. We need to be bold to take authority in Jesus' name over things like this. Not in our own power, but quietly depending on Him to bring things back into control.

I was able to get some important things done today. Then

my friend, Darla, took me out to dinner, and we enjoyed a very nice visit. If I am able to write in a way that is both honest and entertaining it is because of Darla and Maggie—both of whom were members, together with me, of our writing group. These two women were the midwives that helped my writing be born. Their friendship is something I treasure. I'm so grateful that I was able to stay in Milan a little while so that I could spend time with friends like Darla.

This evening I will go visit that South American mission church that the couple on the subway frequent. It could be a divine appointment. I will have lunch tomorrow with Suzy and Sally—sisters who have become sisters to me. I am invited to all their family functions. They are my best friends in Italy. I call one Mamma because she fusses over me with motherly attention and love. (Note to Mom: You don't have to worry about me when I'm here, because God has cloned you in Suzy to watch over me here!) God is good!

## Russia

The world's largest country, covering nine time zones, Russia has millions of poor and unemployed people, and the economy suffers from a huge budget deficit, entrenched corruption and bribery, a crumbling and aged infrastructure, limited foreign investment, low productivity, and alarming demographic decline. Each year the population drops by over 500,000, due to many sad factors: one of the world's lowest birthrates; one of the world's highest abortion rates (many of which result in the mother's death); inefficient, underfunded, and costly—and therefore inaccessible—healthcare; one of the world's highest rates of alcoholism (cheap, illegal (and often poisonous) vodka, and disease, homicide, and suicide factor into alcoholism rates); drug addiction (over 2.5 million addicts), with Russian mafia involvement; and Europe's highest and fastest-rising rate of HIV/AIDS (mostly among the youth). Millions of Russians claim membership in the Russian Orthodox Church without actually believing in God. Cults and sects, both Eastern and Western, and belief in the paranormal are common. Outreach is needed for the youth and children, prisoners (over 825,000—one of the least-reached and most responsive groups), Muslims, Jews, Romani (Gypsies), and Chinese.

Pray for unity and a vision for outreach throughout this vast land. (Operation World, pgs. 705-718.)

## Faith Trip - Days 38 & 39
## A Hostel Environment

*Every great movement of God can be traced to a kneeling figure.*
*D.L. Moody*

Greetings from Switzerland! I had one last appointment in Milan: coffee with Samuele, who shared with me thoughts and prayer points about his ministry. Then about noon I took the highway north to Switzerland. As you remember, Bob and Jill are time-sharing the Duchess (they will use her during the summer months). We arranged to meet at a missionary base in Switzerland.

I left Milan in the blazing heat, and predicted to reach 38° (100° Fahrenheit!)—a really good time to go to Switzerland! Almost as soon as I reached the border of Switzerland, the temperature cooled. Then in the first valley, the temperature dropped so suddenly that it was almost as if I had gone from summer back to early spring. The Duchess lost momentum going uphill, but when I got to the San Gottardo Tunnel, she did great at holding her speed. And for the rest of the trip, she was a champ. She's a dream to drive, even on a drizzly Swiss highway, and not bad even in the city. When I reached the base a local bank announced the temperature to be 19° (66° Fahrenheit!). Relief!

Bob and Michael (their five year old middle child) met me at a gas station. Michael wanted to be the first of the kids to ride in the Duchess, so he climbed in and buckled-up. And

Bob led us to the base, which I would probably never have found on my own. There were lots of people and lots of activity. Most of the missionaries were young people, 30-35 years younger than me, and just back from various outreaches, lending an exciting dynamic to the place. Many of them had children, which added even more fun to the atmosphere.

I had a chance to connect with a group just back from Bulgaria. They told me about the situation, which is similar to what I had observed in Romania. They were as astonished as I was by the contrast between the Roma (gypsies) and the rest of Bulgarian society. I don't know that there could be a wider cultural gap than the Roma and European society.

The hospitality director at the base told me that I had only one night in the hospitality center because there's another team coming in today, and they need my room. So I checked out this morning without knowing where I'm going. There happened to be a girl, Margie, who was going to Bern, so we rode the bus to town together and then the train. Since Margie is Swiss, she knew how to ask directions and everything in German. Most of the younger people speak English, but this gave her the chance to feel important and helpful. And she did help me. She helped me buy a phone. Vodafone apparently doesn't have a presence in Switzerland, so I had to buy a phone, and the process was almost as complicated as applying for citizenship. Margie also helped me get the last bed at a youth hostel—the rest of the city was booked solid because there are several conventions in town.

My first experience in a youth hostel was last summer with Kevin in Poland. It was bad. I had told myself at the time that I would never again stay in a hostel. What made it bad was sleeping in a mixed sex dormitory of 12 beds. That meant that there was a great deal of disorder and drunkenness. Each night I had been woken up by drunken boys coming in at three in the morning, stumbling over the stuff they had left all over the floor, turning on lights, talking loudly, and then falling into bed to sleep it off while I lay there wide-awake with no hope of getting back to sleep.

But today I had no choice, the city is booked solid. This hostel is not like that at all—thank God! I'm in a women's dormitory of six beds.

~ **The Next Morning** ~

My dorm mates kept their things neatly put away, and although they returned late, they were very considerate and did not wake me. What a difference! However, I woke this morning with a migraine attack so severe that for a while I didn't think I would be able to climb down from my upper bunk. I eventually did manage to get down. I was feeling so sick that I almost asked for another night in the hostel. But after a light breakfast of tea and dry toast (all I could manage because of the nausea), I felt a little better. In fact, I felt just good enough to get myself to the train station and buy a ticket to return to Milan. Even when I'm not feeling my best, God is good! No matter what I'm going through, He is always good, and He is always worthy to be praised!

## Switzerland

High mountainous land with a strong policy of non-involvement and neutrality, Switzerland is well-known for banking and tourism. Despite its political and geographical isolation, Switzerland struggles with many of the same social and spiritual problems as its neighbors: wealth, comfort, political apathy, and the decline of the Catholic Church have created an atmosphere of vague religiosity, and in the vacuum the younger generation is turning to Eastern religions and the occult; low birthrate and rapidly-aging population plus immigration equals the changing face of the Swiss. The population is now more than 22% foreign, from more than 100 nationalities, many of whom are Muslim and largely unintegrated.

Pray for sensitive and effective, youth-oriented outreach that will turn the tide and bring renewed vitality to the Swiss spiritual life. (Operation World, pgs. 799-802.)

# Faith Trip - Days 40 & 41
## A Gift From God!

*Sons are a heritage from the Lord, children a reward from*
*Him.*
*Psalm 127:3*

Kevin is at the end of his visit to Italy, so he invited me to
come visit him again in Florence. And in the morning I
woke up to the wonderful news that I am a grandmother.
My grandson was born on the very day predicted: 4th of
July—American Independence Day. He's beautiful. Kevin
is thrilled to be an uncle. We talked on Skype with Josh, his
brother, the new daddy. My mom (now a
great-grandmother) said: "He's our little firecracker!" It
was a fantastic blessing to be with my son when news of
our newest family member came!

We spent the rest of the day spreading the news and
enjoying each other's company. God is good!

This morning I left Florence floating on the joy of my
grandson's birth and my wonderful visit with Kevin. It was
a lovely break.

Back to ministry now, I am in a small town in northern
Italy, visiting Bethany. She had invited me out to dinner
the night before the Faith Trip began (see Day 0). When we
had first met, she had been led by the Holy Spirit to sell all
her possessions and move here to help this church. What
she did not know at the time is that the church is facing
some difficulties and challenges. The pastors are dedicated

servants of God, but for some reason their flock is having serious problems with gossip, jealousy, and worldliness, despite their own constant prayer and teaching about the dangers of these behaviors. Bethany sees these problems more starkly with the clarity of fresh eyes, while the pastors, being tender-hearted, tend to see with loving, parental eyes. As she told me about these problems, I kept saying, "We need to pray about this." We did pray. And this morning as we discussed these things over breakfast, and we prayed again.

## United Kingdom

The UK includes England, Northern Ireland, Scotland, Wales, the Isle of Man, and the Channel Islands. The "freedoms" of the 1960's led to social disaster and spiritual decline. The tradition of Judeo-Christian that has so long characterized the UK has dissolved been labeled as "intolerant" and become marginalized and replaced by multi-cultural pluralism that embraces Islam, Astrology, New Age, the occult and old-world paganism (Druid/Wicca). An overall feeling of discouragement and cynicism about the future, and the seeming impotence of politicians (fueled by media) has resulted in serious problems: violent crime, alcohol and drug abuse, sexually transmitted diseases, immorality, prostitution, illegitimacy and abortion rates, gambling addiction, and high personal debt. There are an estimated 600,000 to 900,000 illegal immigrants, leading to problems with integration and

153

criminal and terrorist threats. Youth are also a particular concern, as the UK "leads" Europe in: teenage sexual activity, sexually transmitted diseases, teen pregnancy, abortion, binge drinking, drug abuse, violent crime, and non-participation in either school or the workplace.

Pray for strong unity within the Body of Christ, and a commitment to reach out to all the UK's people with the love and hope of Jesus Christ. (Operation World, pgs. 850-860.)

## Faith Trip - Day 42
## Missional? Part II

*I have but one passion—it is He, it is He alone. The world is the field, and the field is the world; and henceforth that country shall be my home where I can be most used in winning souls for Christ.*
*Count Nikolaus Ludwig von Zinzendorf*

This morning at the Sunday service I noticed that this church is probably the most seeker *in*sensitive church I've ever attended. The church is difficult to find, there are no greeters, no bulletins, the songs are difficult to follow if you don't know them because the words are neither projected nor given to you on handouts. The visitor that does manage to find the church is singled-out and asked to stand in front with the pastor while he asks you what you're doing here (the treatment I got), all done very kindly, but very daunting for a new person. All that is enough to send most seekers running out the door. But then there's also the sermon, which Bethany tells me, over 80% of the time always includes the need to fight our sin nature. Sure enough, the pastor preached about our sin nature, and concluded his sermon by stating, "Without suffering there is no personal growth." The final song was a dirge. On the way home, I wondered aloud how many of the members had gone home to flog themselves. We giggled, but the hard truth is that this church is in serious trouble, and is very unlikely ever to grow.

What to do? I didn't come to criticize the church or its pastors, but to help it. Bethany assures me that at least one of these things will change: the church has been offered some land for a building. But that could take a while.

I think this situation is going to need a lot of prayer. And I believe that both Bethany and I were called here to do exactly that: pray, pray, pray. She is gently advising the pastors about what we see going on here, and standing with them in prayer. But they rebuff her observations and advice with a dismissive, "Things are different here in Italy." Things *are* different in Italy, but not the need to be more sensitive to those seeking a relationship with Jesus. Both of us feel the urgency for more prayer over the situation.

## Serbia & Kosovo

Mostly Orthodox Serbia sees itself as the defender of Europe and Christianity against Muslim aggression. The Kosovar Albanian population is mostly Muslim. Communist domination, the breakup of Yugoslavia, and the Balkan wars; UN trade sanctions, and NATO military intervention have greatly weakened the economy. In Kosovo, the economy is actually shrinking, with unemployment at 70%. Ethnic/religious hatred, nationalism, and greed contributed to the violence and "ethnic cleansing" of the Milosevic era.

Pray that communal hatreds might be resolved, that lasting peace, not dependent on foreign military involvement, be established; and for an end to religious hatred in the spirit of true Christian love. (Operation World, pgs. 734-737.)

## Faith Trip - Days 43 & 44
## Redeemed!

*There has never been a spiritual awakening in any country
or locality that did not begin in united prayer.*
*A.T. Pierson*

Greetings from southern Germany! My cousin, Max,
moved here two weeks ago, and he invited me to come for
a visit. I agreed and bought tickets without praying about it
first. When I did pray about it, God told me He would not
bless this trip because I hadn't asked Him first. I spent an
hour or so praying, begging God to please bless my trip,
and He finally agreed, and said that He would "redeem"
the trip.

On the train to Germany I was in a compartment with two
Arab men. One was a lawyer who was just learning
English, and the other taught English back in Saudi Arabia.
The teacher was very talkative and curious about my life
both in Italy and in the US. He was politely interested, and
never tried to engage me in debate about religion (nor I
him!). The thing is that it would be useless to try and argue
somebody into Heaven. So I merely shared with him the
hope I have. Then he opened the book of Mary from the
Koran for me to read on his iPhone. I was surprised to see
that Muslims also believe in the virgin birth of Jesus.

He also shared with me some interesting cultural
information about courtship and marriage. He said that his
(future) mother-in-law came to visit his mother, and
between the two of them they decided to consider a match

between their children. Then on the next visit she brought her daughter (his future wife), and his mother looked the girl over, and talked with her. Then he met her for the first time at a dinner held by the two families, but never got closer to her than three meters, and he never spoke to her, nor her to him. This dinner formalized the match, but the marriage contract was sealed when he came to her house, bringing the equivalent of €5,000. He gave the money to his future mother-in-law to give to his fiancée so that she could buy a wedding dress and some articles for the house. Finally, there was the wedding, with the celebration that lasted five days. And still they had never exchanged words! When this was all over, then he took her home and she was his wife. He said that after a while love comes. They have three children: two girls and a boy, (ages ten, eight, and five). I asked if he would arrange marriages for his children, and he said, "That's woman's work, but yes, they will have arranged marriages, too."

He also said that in Saudi Arabia a man can have up to four wives, and that his father has four wives. I asked him if he was going to take more wives and he laughed and said that wives are expensive. He said that he loves his father's other wives like aunts, but feels mother-love only for his own mother.

On the train returning to Italy I met a nice German woman who was traveling for the first time since her husband's death in February. Her destination was a castle in Italy near the border of Austria. Like the English teacher, she was happy for an opportunity to practice her English. The castle is owned by her friend who had been widowed a few years ago.

I had a nice visit with Max, and told him about my Faith Trip and about the ministry. I am glad that I got to see him. And I'm glad that God "redeemed" the trip, though it's probably best to ask God before making plans. God is good!

## Germany

Reunification in 1989 caused Germany's strong economy to stumble, and while it still remains Europe's economic leader, unemployment remains a problem especially in the east. Humanism and destructive criticism of the Bible in the 19th Century weakened churches and opened the door to compromise and eventual pagan Nazi tyranny. Post WWII dynamics accelerated the secularization and de-Christianization of society, creating the marginalization of and hostility toward Christianity, the rise of false religious teachings (New Age, the occult, Satanism, and pre-Christian paganism), and mental illnesses in record numbers (including clinical depression and suicide—the second-largest killer of 15-29 year olds). Gruesome crimes and killings are also on the rise in the absence of any kind of moral foundation. Much of the German population remains unreached.

Pray for unity among believers, and for church-planting initiatives throughout the country. (Operation World, pgs. 359-364.)

### Faith Trip - Day 45
### Mission Accomplished!

*He is no fool who gives what he cannot keep to gain what
he cannot lose.*
*Jim Eliot*

I returned to Milan late last night, and slept like a rock.
This morning I woke at about eight—which is late for me. I
woke up thinking about how I had made those plans to visit
my cousin without consulting God first. As I was praying, I
asked God about all the other plans I've made for the rest
of the summer and into fall: plans to visit friends, plans to
return to the US and see my grandbaby, etc. I told God that
I want everything I do to be pleasing to Him, and that I
hoped I hadn't made any other plans that would have to be
"redeemed." Then God gently assured me that all those
other plans had been made motivated by love. Whereas the
plan to visit my cousin contained an element of
selfishness—which is the opposite of love. He said that He
had redeemed that trip because my desire to see my cousin
wasn't completely selfish. He said that it's best to pray
before making plans, but that if love—genuine, pure, godly
love—was my motivation, then I will always be moving in
step with Him. It all keeps coming back to Look, Listen,
Love.

And then He told me that my Faith Trip has ended. My
lesson in following His instructions has been learned.

Although I started this Faith Trip feeling not scared, but
perhaps anxious, now I'm feeling a little sad that it's over.

It has been a wonderful adventure full of surprises and blessings and new friends all along the way. My life, which appears to be solitary, is in fact filled with family and friends who love me—both here throughout Europe and also throughout North America. I am rich beyond belief in the love of family and friends—the only riches that really count or last. I have also learned the valuable lesson of relaxing and floating above troubles, resting completely in God Almighty who is on my side.

God is good! Never doubt it! God is good!

## Slovenia

Slovenia is the most prosperous of the former Yugoslav republics. The three main Christian groups (Catholic, Orthodox, and Lutheran) lack spiritual vitality and are rapidly declining into irrelevance, while agnosticism, New Age, and various Eastern religions are increasing along with a general spiritual apathy. Important Christian resources are in short supply: Christian literature, a modern translation of the Slovenian Bible, and modern translations of the works of Primoz Trubar, the Slovene Protestant reformer.

Pray for these works and for church planting efforts that will bear great fruit. (Operation World, pgs. 749-751.)

## Epilogue
## Follow-Up Thoughts

*In no other way can the believer become as fully involved with God's work, especially the work of world evangelism, as in intercessory prayer.*
*Dick Eastman*

As I said in the introduction, I always felt that there was something special, something important for my life: I was called from the womb like Jeremiah (Jeremiah 1:5) ". . . set apart for a special work" (NCV). That's not to say that I am special or extraordinary, but I serve an extraordinary and amazing God. All these things you've just read about are because of His work in me.

Now it's your turn. I have two very important questions to ask you:

**1.   Have you made a decision for Jesus Christ?** If not, now is the time to do so. Quit sitting on the fence, waiting for a sign—you're not going to get one. This book found its way into your hands for the singular purpose of bringing you to this moment of decision. And know this: putting off a decision is the same as saying NO. God wants to take away your sins—all of them—and give you abundant (full-to-overflowing) life. Abundant life isn't a thing just for the everlasting adventure of Heaven, but also for here and now. But He's not going to force anything on you, not even His love. It's up to you to ask for it. Asking is as simple as this:

162

You're right, God, I need You. Please take away my sins. Thank You for sending Your Son, Jesus, to save me and to give me abundant life. Please help me to live a life that is pleasing to You. Amen.

If you just prayed that prayer: Welcome to the family! Be sure to speak with God often and honestly. At first it may feel odd, a little like talking to your invisible friend, but with time you'll find this Friend is very real. Listen, too. He speaks audibly or in your spirit at times, or through other people, and sometimes in dreams or in visions, but mostly He speaks through the Bible. If you think God has communicated something strange to you, check the Bible because God will never, ever tell you to do something that is contrary to His Word. Reading the Bible is the best way to get to know God, and to know what God wants you to do. You will also need to find a mature Christian friend (of your same sex) to disciple you (that is, to help you learn how to live as a Christian). Church or home group attendance is important because we need each other, so find other Christians to get together with on a regular basis. But don't expect to find perfect people because just like you, we are all works in progress.

## Spain and Gibraltar

Since 1978 Spain has gone from dictatorship to liberty, poverty to wealth, isolation to integration, religious discrimination to religious liberty—more than 30 years. However, this transformation brought decadent behaviors and hedonistic lifestyles and the resulting depression, drug and gambling addictions, debt, prostitution, abortion, and spiritual confusion (rejection of absolute truth, dabbling in occult, New Age, Jehovah's Witnesses, and Mormons. Gibraltar (nominally independent of both British and Spanish control) is strategically placed for outreach because many tourists visit (especially Spaniards buying duty-free goods), several thousand Moroccan guest workers, Jewish and Hindu communities.

Pray for outreach to all the Spanish, Gibraltarians, and tourists, and particularly the largely unreached: the Basques, Muslims, Chinese, drug addicts, young people, the elderly and retirees. (Operation World, pgs. 369-370; 764-769.)

# Epilogue, Part II
## Your Calling

*If Jesus be God and died for me, then no sacrifice can be*
*too great for me to make for Him.*
C.T. Studd

**2. What has God called you to do?** If you can't answer
that question, you need to investigate and discover your
calling. Your calling is different from your purpose. Your
purpose is the same as my purpose—the same as
everyone's purpose: to know and to love the Lord God,
your Creator, and to bring glory to His name. Your calling
is something specific to you.

One way to discover your calling is to investigate the
spiritual gifts. "We have different gifts, according to the
grace given us," (Romans 12:6a). Take some time to read
Romans 12, I Corinthians 12, and Ephesians 4:11-12. Take
a spiritual gifts test and discover your spiritual gifting.

Once you know your gifting, seek God and search your
heart. I was once afraid that God would call me to ministry
in the jungle—a place I, personally, have no desire to ever
go to. First, I like sleeping under a roof, on a bed, a couch,
or at the very least a mattress on the floor. Plus, I really,
really appreciate living in the age of flush toilets and warm
showers, and I'm not going to give that up unless I
absolutely must. Second, I am a complete sissy when it
comes to bugs, even the ones that don't bite or sting. At the
Orkin Insect Zoo in Washington, D.C. I had the
opportunity to touch a giant hissing cockroach. The curator
had a box full of them in her lap that she was offering to the

children around her. Each of these children held a cockroach, letting it crawl from one hand to the other and even up their arms. She held one out for me to touch. I was a 45-year-old mother of two, terrified of bugs. I reached out my hand, but I couldn't bring myself to touch it. I was pretty sure that if I did, I would probably scream. But God didn't call me to the jungle. If I was called to the jungle, I would have the desire to go and live in the jungle. Your desire, if it's not selfish, is a big clue to your calling.

Pray about your desire and if it's a call from God, answer the call. He's calling you to a life that's better in *every* way than the ordinary life the world has assigned to you: fun, adventure, discovery, freedom. Where? Only God can answer that. Your ministry might be right there where you are now or it may require a move. Either way, it's going to mean joining God in whatever work He's already doing.

"Oh, but I can't," you might be thinking. What is stopping you? Your job? Your family? Lack of money? Has it ever occurred to you that the *reason* you're struggling financially right now is because you're saying NO to God? He loves to bless and prosper His children (Psalm 34:8-10), but He also disciplines His children in love (Hebrews 12:5-80). He blocks your path with thorn bushes (Hosea 2:6) and allures you, speaking tenderly (Hosea 2:14) to get you to change direction. Sometimes making you uncomfortable is the only way to get through to you.

T.S. Eliot said: "When the Christian faith is not only felt, but thought, it has practical results which may be

166

inconvenient[1]." Who said the Christian life is convenient? Jesus certainly didn't! "Foxes have holes and birds of the air have nests, but the Son of Man has no place to lay His head," (Matthew 8:20). Read also Matthew 10:17-37: Jesus said that Christians will be opposed and even persecuted to death by religious leaders, governments, and even by our own family members. But He also promised: "Whoever acknowledges Me before men, I will also acknowledge him before My Father in Heaven," (verse 32). That's not for the sweet by-and-by, that's also for here and now! Jesus is our High Priest, and He is in Heaven pleading with the Father for our sake (Hebrews 4:14-5:10).

Are you ready for adventure? Your own Faith Trip? Every day with God is new and different. It's freeing, fun, exhilarating, but also risky, uncomfortable, and dangerous at times. Bad stuff happens to people who aren't living for Jesus, too. But you have an advantage. Never forget that you have God Almighty as your Companion, your Help, your Provider, your Comforter, your Defender. He's on your side!

God is good!

## Sweden

High taxation supports an extensive social welfare system

---

[1] T.S. Eliot, Christianity and Culture (Fort Washington, PA: Harvest Books, 1960), 6.

for one of the best standards of living in the world. Only 23 percent of Swedes believe in God, and belief in absolute values or truth is regarded as "intolerance."

Pray for outreach, especially to the youth, the indigenous Saami peoples, immigrants from former Communist nations, Muslims (largely unintegrated), and East and South Asian peoples. (Operation World, pgs. 795-798.)

## Faith Trip - A Month Later
## Back at the Beach

*If a commission by an earthly king is considered an honor,*
*how can a commission by a*
*Heavenly King be considered a sacrifice?*
*David Livingstone*

Many of the people who followed my adventures on the blog and in prayer updates have asked what I've done since the Faith Trip ended.

What I did was to pick up Boo-Boo from the Stefanelli's, and she and I took a nice, long vacation at the beach—thanks to Bob and Jill for the use of their house! Although I've learned the lessons of Look, Listen, Love, and of Relaxing and floating, by now you probably know that I can't keep still for long. This book that you hold in your hands is what I've been doing for the past month.

I've been following a daily routine of writing in the morning (when my mind is sharpest) and taking an afternoon swim (OK, float) in the sea. I've been joined here by Suzy and Sally, and others have dropped by, too. Suzy, the "Little Mother of Everyone" has taken over cooking, cleaning, laundry, and grocery shopping tasks, which has freed me up to concentrate on writing.

As I face the obstacle of proofreading and editing, I hope that somehow I can count on the help of Darla and Maggie. Our schedules would appear to say otherwise, but who knows? Perhaps God will open up a way that I can meet with them after all.

Suzy and I took a couple of day trips: one to a small mountain village where my ministry partner's great-grandfather was born and the other to L'Aquila. Both trips were for the purpose of prayer. While walking through L'Aquila's earthquake-devastated center I came to a church with a skeleton carved over the doorway. It occurred to me to wonder how many of the victims of the earthquake had entered through that "death door." I prayed, taking authority over the spirit of death and breaking its hold over L'Aquila. Then I spoke life over that once-great city.

Another thing I've been doing this month is reading. God has put some amazing, great books into my hands. I've been learning more about myself and my place in this world and in God's kingdom.

One thing He's shown me this past month is the lies of the enemy that I've believed about myself. I was molested by a neighbor when I was seven years old. He had lured me into his bedroom while my brother and his son played together. I had avoided rape by saying, "I hear my mother calling!" and running home. But feelings of guilt and shame kept my mouth shut. I didn't tell my parents about it until almost 20 years later because I believed the enemy's lie that it was my fault. Looking back now I wish I could tell that little girl (myself) how strong and brave and clever and good she is.

My innocence died that day. I grew up ashamed, hating my

vulnerability, and thus hating myself. I learned to hide myself behind all sorts of busy work, like a true resident of Marthaland (see Day 36). All the work I was doing was good, worthwhile stuff: teaching Sunday School, reading to children at the school and at the library (at one time I had an audience of probably 300 children throughout the week), substitute teaching at the local Christian Academy, teaching adult education Creative Writing, and taking all sorts of classes to improve myself. All those activities were to hide from the pain of my broken heart. Overeating was also a way of hiding from my broken heart. And I'm sure that you can understand now why it was so hard for me to wait by the sea for the camper to be ready. During that time, I had nothing to distract me from myself.

Last night I heard a sermon about the creative power of words. "The tongue has the power of life and death, and those who love it will eat its fruit," (Proverbs 18:21). For good or for evil, our words have power: life and death. And the preacher read us Psalm 1:1. I'm sure I've read it dozens of times, but now I really understand: "Blessed is the man who does not walk in the counsel of the wicked or stand in the way of sinners or sit in the seat of mockers." He said that "walking in the counsel of the wicked" is accepting a label that is contrary to God's Word. For example, his teachers told his parents that he was good with math, but would never be much good with reading or writing. He said that he decided not to accept that labeling, and instead to see what the Word of God says about him: "I praise You because I am fearfully and wonderfully made; Your works are wonderful, I know that full well," (Psalm 139:14). Now this boy who the teachers said would "never be much good

171

at reading or writing" has written five books.

That reminded me of six years ago, when I told my doctor I was having trouble losing weight, she said, "I wouldn't worry about it, Ms. Brown. You're just plump." I don't have to accept that labeling! God says that I'm fearfully and wonderfully made! That body shame I mentioned (Day 26) didn't come from God. You've seen by now that I am very honest about my faults, but at the same time, I realize that I need to be careful not to be reinforcing bad labels over myself. It's a fine line. Writing honestly, hoping to get a laugh of recognition, is yet another way to hide my broken heart.

From now on I'm taking my broken heart to Jesus who says:

> The Spirit of the Sovereign Lord is on Me because the Lord has anointed Me to preach good news to the poor. *He has sent me to bind up the brokenhearted*, to proclaim freedom for the captives and release from darkness for the prisoners, to proclaim the year of the Lord's favor and the day of vengeance of our God, to comfort all who mourn, and provide for those who grieve in Zion—*to bestow on them a crown of beauty instead of ashes*, the oil of gladness instead of mourning, and a garment of praise instead of a spirit of despair. They will be called oaks of righteousness, a planting of the Lord *for the display of His splendor* (Isaiah 61:3, emphasis mine).

172

I am trading in those old ashes and all the rotten lies the devil has told me. I am beautiful. I display His splendor. I am beloved. I am worthy of love. I am worth the effort. I am not afraid to be vulnerable. I am precious. I am a royal daughter of King Jesus. I am a royal bride. And I know God. I know that "He who began a good work in [me] will carry it on to completion until the day of Christ Jesus," (Philippians 1:6).

God is good!

Here's a list of excellent books that I've read recently:

- Wild at Heart by John Eldredge (about men's souls)

- Captivating by John and Stasi Eldredge (companion book to Wild at Heart, about women's souls—I recommend that both men and women read both—especially if you are married or thinking of marrying)

- The Next Christians: The Good News About the End of Christian America by Gabe Lyons (about being missional)

- Absolute Surrender by Andrew Murray (about letting God lead)

- The Supernatural Ways of Royalty: Discovering Your Rights and Privileges of Being a Son or Daughter of God by Kris Vallotton & Bill

Johnson (about understanding who you are in God's kingdom)

- Europe: Restoring Hope by Deborah Meroff (about how and where missions work is being done in Europe)

- Operation World by Jason Mandryk (a valuable resource for praying purposefully for the world country-by-country)

## Ukraine

Children at risk is a severe problem, with tens of thousands of street children, over 100,000 children living in orphanages, and many others in precarious living situations. Many of these suffer health complications from Chernobyl. The majority of orphans will become involved in drugs, crime, or prostitution. Ukraine has a strong Christian legacy. It was the "Bible Belt" of the Soviet sphere, and suffered 130 years of persecution in which millions of Christians were killed. There is nominally freedom of religion, but the reality is that Ukraine straddles the divide between East and West, Orthodox and Catholic, and this makes for divisions and tension. Cults are a serious issue, particularly: Jehovah's Witnesses, Hare Krishna, indigenous pagan groups, and Mormons.

Pray for unity within the Body of Christ, and for outreach that will bring hope to the children and the marginalized peoples: Jews, foreign immigrants, and the mostly Muslim Crimean Tatars. (Operation World, pgs. 844-847.)

## Acknowledgments
## The Folks Who God Used to Make the Faith Trip
## Possible

*Intercession is truly universal work for the Christian. No place is closed to intercessory prayer. No continent—no nation—no organization—no city—no office. There is no power on earth that can keep intercession out.*
*Richard Halverson*

I want to remember all the people who have been supporting me in prayer, hospitality, and many other ways:

- My prayer partners. Their prayers have sustained me through the difficult times, protected me from unknown and untold dangers and hazards, and helped me to keep on the right path. I am very, very grateful for all prayers made on my behalf and in the name of friendship.

- Raffa and Deivi (whose door is always open and couch is always available for me!), Juan David, Filomena; Gianni, Eddy and Adriana, Valentina and Andrea; Nelly and Jairo and Emanuel; Bertha and Dara; Nicoletta, Alejandro, Francesca (a role model!); Barnaba and Jennavave; Silvia and Pasquale; Giuseppe and Genesis and Luz, and my English students from Scegligesùschool: Rostand, Agnese, Stefano, and Bruna (the Blond Bomb!); Tina and Adrianna (my fantastic cell group leaders), and all the pastors and many, many friends at Sabaoth (my family on this

176

continent!); Saidè and Matteo, Orietta and Mauro (and Daniele), Clara (always ready with a great meal and a warm bed!), Rita and Davide, Simone and Gabriella, Loredana and Martina, Micky and Jonathan, Davide and Mary, and all the rest of the dear people of the church at Biella (a piece of my heart will always be there with you all!); Horst and Amparo and all the wonderful folks at Gesù È La Risposta; Sergio and Franca (God's Friends!) and Paolo, Ergian, and Annamaria and Cristiana (who chose Christ and Him alone!); the fabulous Goldney Five; Guiseppe and Cristiana; Evodia and Lajos, their 5 precious children and Evodia's parents—true pillars of the Church in Romania; the amazing Sally (a valuable friend and role model!); and special mention goes to Debbie, who has stuck with me when others would have given up, who has helped in ways too numerous to mention, who has sacrificed a lot to make this vision a reality, who is not only a fantastic friend, but a ministry partner who is truly worth her weight in gold.

- My family: my super-supportive Mom (the best blessing of all!); Jeff and Jessica and Orion, and Tim and Maureen (the next generation and the hope for a bright future); Terry and Lynn and Houston; Ann, David and Kathy, Dewey and Leticia, Amanda, David, Pat and Ted, Gunnar, Janice, and special mention for Fleur, who has been a dear friend through all life's ups and downs over the last 48 years (a friend who "sticks closer than a sister," to paraphrase Proverbs 18:24).

- Foundation, my church back in Bastrop, Texas: Pastors Chris and Melissa, and all their family, they are wise far beyond their years, funny, supportive, godly, wonderful people; Veronica and Stan, Brooke, Linda, Yolanda and Luis, Isahiah, LaShae, Eric, Ashleigh, Ashley, Shelby, Lori, Chase, Jolene, and especially Chantz and Renee and Brodie and Brett, missionaries who are friends and role-models.

- Friends on both continents who always have something encouraging to say: Mary, Alicia, Maria, Gary, Nancy, Sally, Renee, Orietta, Tanja, Debbie, Tina, Eddy, Francesca, Ann, Shiv, Maurizio, Davide and Cristina, Giovanna, Lesley, Eleonora, Nicoletta, Cristian, Francisco, Melissa, Ruth, Ashleigh, Ashley, Shelby, Catherine, Lori, Sergio, Fleur, and with special mention for Laurie (and Don and their stadium-full of kids and grandkids).

Thank you for your prayers and support! God bless your socks off (as we say in Texas!)!

### Russia

The world's largest country, covering nine time zones,

Russia has millions of poor and unemployed people, and the economy suffers from a huge budget deficit, entrenched corruption and bribery, a crumbling and aged infrastructure, limited foreign investment, low productivity, and alarming demographic decline. Each year the population drops by over 500,000, due to many sad factors: one of the world's lowest birthrates; one of the world's highest abortion rates (many of which result in the mother's death); inefficient, underfunded, and costly—and therefore inaccessible—healthcare; one of the world's highest rates of alcoholism (cheap, illegal (and often poisonous) vodka, and disease, homicide, and suicide factor into alcoholism rates); drug addiction (over 2.5 million addicts), with Russian mafia involvement; and Europe's highest and fastest-rising rate of HIV/AIDS (mostly among the youth). Millions of Russians claim membership in the Russian Orthodox Church without actually believing in God. Cults and sects, both Eastern and Western, and belief in the paranormal are common. Outreach is needed for the youth and children, prisoners (over 825,000—one of the least-reached and most responsive groups), Muslims, Jews, Romani (Gypsies), and Chinese.

Pray for unity and a vision for outreach throughout this vast land. (Operation World, pgs. 705-718.)